HOW TO SING

Lilli Lehmann

Translated from the German
by
RICHARD ALDRICH

New Revised and Supplemented Edition
translated by
CLARA WILLENBÜCHER

DOVER PUBLICATIONS, INC.
NEW YORK

Bibliographical Note

This Dover edition, first published in 1993, is a republication of the third revised and supplemented edition, 1924, of the work first published in English in 1902 (all three editions published by The Macmillan Company, New York). The original German version, *Meine Gesangskunst* [My Art of Song], was first published in Berlin in 1902; third German edition, 1922. The original frontispiece has been omitted.

Library of Congress Cataloging-in-Publication Data

Lehmann, Lilli, 1848–1929.
    [Meine Gesangskunst. English]
    How to sing / Lilli Lehmann ; translated from the German by Richard Aldrich. — New rev. and supplemented ed. / translated by Clara Willenbücher.
        p.   cm.
    "An unabridged republication of the third revised and supplemented edition, 1924, of the work first published in English in 1902 (all three editions published by the Macmillan Company, New York)"—T.p. verso.
    ISBN 0-486-27501-9 (pbk.)
    1. Singing—Methods. I. Title.
MT840.L42   1993
783'.04—dc20
                                    92-43865
                                         CIP
                                       MN

Manufactured in the United States of America
Dover Publications, Inc., 31 East 2nd Street, Mineola, N.Y. 11501

Preface to the Third Revised Edition

IT were well if pupils, yes and professional singers, too, were conscious of just one thing, that the singing tone is to be found in the resonance of one's own body, in the chest and head resonances, and not in the auditorium into which the singer strives solely to project his breath to produce big tones.

Our body is simultaneously the instrument and the resonance box upon which we have to learn to play. Our muscles are the strings which we must learn to tune, tighten and loosen, one to the other, and our soul is the director of our art.

As the pipes of an organ, through their form and air pressure, give that instrument the possibility of endless variations in tone, range, and means of expression, so we, too, must create for our tones and ranges living forms with our vocal organs and resonances.

As a clock is wound to set all parts of the work in action, so we singers must put together all our coöperative organs and muscles into a well-joined instrument, set it in action, and keep it in activity.

In the shortest song, the shortest phrase, we have to remake our instrument a thousand times over and keep it going, for the slightest inattention or the slightest injury to the form—which is apt to happen in the pronunciation—is liable to mutilate the artistically set instrument or its tone coloring.

Our vocal art is a marvel just as our instrument is one, and a beautiful human voice which is so blessed as to be able to give forth that which stirs our hearts is an incomparable, glorious marvel. We singers are in duty bound to become closely acquainted with this instrument in order to serve humanity with an ideal art.

LILLI LEHMANN.

GRUNEWALD, January, 1922.

Contents

Publisher's Note

THE GREAT German soprano Lilli Lehmann, born in Würzburg in 1848, made her operatic debut in Prague in 1865. She took part in the first complete cycle of Wagner's *Ring des Nibelungen*, at Bayreuth in 1876. In 1880 she made her London debut, singing the role of Violetta, and in 1882 Vienna heard her for the first time. After a fruitful career at the Berlin Opera she went to New York and in the winter of 1885 she made her debut at the Metropolitan as Carmen. During her first season at the Metropolitan her roles included Bertha (*Le Prophète*), Marguerite (*Faust*), Irene (*Rienzi*) and Venus (*Tannhäuser*). Lehmann's astonishingly broad repertoire extended from light coloratura roles of Bellini and Offenbach to the dramatic roles—particularly those of Wagner—for which she was universally admired. Toward the end of her career she was closely associated with the Salzburg Festival, achieving many successes there and eventually serving as the Festival's artistic director. She continued to appear in recital until 1920 when she retired from a triumphant fifty-five year career. She died in 1929.

Lilli Lehmann began her teaching activities in 1891 and counted among her many notable students the Swedish-American mezzo-soprano Olive Fremstad and the American soprano Geraldine Farrar. Lehmann's own extraordinary repertoire (over one hundred seventy roles), her superb technical mastery and psychological understanding of roles ranging from Wagner and Mozart to Donizetti and Verdi, and the sheer length of her career, testify to the validity of her philosophy and practices as set forth in the present volume.

MOTTO: Acquiring artistic technique is always associated with exaggerations, for isn't it necessary to make others hear, see, and understand, in spacious halls, the singer's own fine feeling for something? The finer the feeling, the more complicated it is. Artistic technique must acquire the harmony of the beautiful through the æstheticism of the soul, and may through it only become—apparently—natural again.

My Purpose

MY purpose is to discuss simply, practically, and in a comprehensible manner such sensations known in singing as singing "open," "covered," "dark," "nasal," "in the head" or "in the neck," "forward" or "back," and particularly my own sensations based on a thorough and precise knowledge. These expressions correspond to our sensations in singing; but they are unintelligible as long as the causes of those sensations are unknown, and each one has a different idea of their meaning. Many singers try their whole lives long to produce them and never succeed. This happens because science understands too little of singing, the singer too little of science. I mean that the physiological explanations of the highly complicated processes of singing are not plainly enough put for the singer, who must depend on his vocal sensations. Scientific men are not at all agreed as to the exact functions of the several organs, and the fewest singers are informed on the subject. Every serious artist has a sincere desire to help others reach the goal—the goal toward which all singers are striving: to sing well and beautifully.

The true art of song has always been possessed and will always be possessed by such individuals as are dowered by nature with all that is needful for it—that is, healthy vocal organs, uninjured by vicious habits of speech; a good ear, a talent for singing, intelligence, industry, and energy.

In former times eight years were devoted to the study of singing—at the Prague Conservatory, for instance. Most of the mistakes and misunderstandings of the pupil could be discovered before he secured an engagement, and the teacher could spend so much time in correcting them that the pupil learned to pass judgment on himself properly.

But art to-day must be pursued like everything else, by steam. Artists are turned out in factories, that is, in so-called conservatories, or by teachers who give lessons ten or twelve hours a day. In two years they receive a certificate of competence, or at least the teacher's diploma of the factory. The latter, especially, I consider a crime that the state should prohibit.

All the inflexibility and unskilfulness, mistakes and deficiencies, which were formerly disclosed during a long course of study, do not appear now, under the factory system, until the student's public career has begun. There can be no question of correcting them, for there is no time, no teacher, no critic; and the executant has learned nothing, absolutely nothing, whereby he could undertake to distinguish or correct them.

My artistic conscience urges me to disclose all that I have learned and that has become clear to me in the course of my career, for the benefit of art; and to give up my "secrets," which seem to be secrets only because students so rarely pursue the path of proper study to its end. If artists, often such only in name, come to a realization of their deficiencies, they lack only too frequently the courage to acknowledge them to others. Not until we artists all reach the point when we can take counsel with each other about our mistakes and deficiencies, and discuss the means for overcoming them, putting our pride in our pockets, will bad singing and inartistic effort be checked, and our noble art of singing come into its rights again.

My Title to Write on the Art of Song

Rarely are so many desirable and necessary antecedents united as in my case.

The child of two singers, my mother being gifted musically quite out of the common, and active for many years not only as a dramatic singer, but also as a harp virtuoso, I, with my sister Marie, received a very careful musical education, and later a notable course of instruction in singing from her. From my fifth year on I listened daily to singing lessons; from my ninth year I played accompaniments on the pianoforte, sang all the missing parts, in French, Italian, German, and Bohemian; got thoroughly familiar with all the operas, and very soon knew how to tell good singing from bad. Our mother took care, too, that we should hear all the visiting notabilities of that time in opera as well as in concert; and there were many of them every year at the Deutsches Landestheater in Prague.

She herself had found a remarkable singing teacher in the Frankfurt basso, Föppel, and kept her voice noble, beautiful, young, and strong to the end of her life—that is, till her seventy-seventh year—notwithstanding enormous demands upon it and many a blow of fate. She could diagnose a voice infallibly; but required a probation of three to four months to test talent and power of making progress.

I have been on the stage since my eighteenth year, that is, for thirty-four years. In Prague I took part every day in operas, operettas, plays, and farces. Thereafter in Danzig I sang from eighteen to twenty times a month in coloratura and soubrette parts; also in Leipzig, and later, fifteen years in Berlin. In addition I sang in very many oratorios and concerts, and gave lessons now and then.

As long as my mother lived she was my severest critic, never satisfied. Finally I became such for myself. Now fifteen years more have passed, of which I spent eight very exacting ones as a dramatic singer in America, afterward fulfilling engagements as a star, in all languages, in Germany, Austria, Hungary, France, England, and Sweden. Nevertheless my study of singing experienced no retrogression. I kept it up more and more zealously by myself, learned something from everybody, learned to *hear* myself and others.

For many years I have been devoting myself to the important questions relating to singing, and believe that I have finally found what I have been seeking. It has been my endeavor to set down as clearly as possible all that I have learned through zealous, conscientious study by myself and with others, and thereby to offer to my colleagues something that will bring order into the chaos of their methods of singing; something based on science as well as on sensations in singing; something that will bring expressions often misunderstood into clear relation with the exact functions of the vocal organs.

In what I have just said I wish to give a sketch of my career only to show what my voice has endured; and why, notwithstanding the enormous demands I have made upon it, it has lasted so well. One who has sung for a short time, and then has lost his voice, and for this reason becomes a singing teacher, has never sung consciously; it has simply been an accident, and this accident will be repeated, for good or for ill, in his pupils.

The talent in which all the requirements of an artist are united is very rare. Real talent will get along, even with an inferior teacher, in some way or another, while the best teacher cannot produce talent where there is none. Such a teacher, however, will not beguile people with promises that cannot be kept.

My chief attention I devote to artists, whom I can, perhaps, assist in their difficult, but glorious, profession. One is never done with learning; and that is especially true of singers. I earnestly hope that I may leave them something, in my researches, experiences, and studies, that will be of use. I regard it as my duty; and I confide it to all who are striving earnestly for improvement.

GRUNEWALD, October 31, 1900.

Preliminary Practice

ALL who wish to become artists should begin with studies of tone production and the functions of nose, tongue, and palate: with the distinct and flexible pronunciation of all letters, especially of consonants. Not until he has acquired this preliminary study should a singer venture upon practical vocal exercises.

Then it would soon be easy to recognize talent or the lack of it. Many would open their eyes in wonder over the difficulties of learning to sing, and the proletariat of singers would gradually disappear. With them would go the singing conservatories and the bad teachers who, for a living, teach everybody that comes, and promise to make everybody a great artist.

The best way is for pupils to learn preparatory books by heart, and make drawings. In this way they will get the best idea of the vocal organs, and learn their functions by sensation as soon as they begin to sing. The pupil should be subjected to strict examinations.

Of what consists artistic singing?

Of a clear understanding, first and foremost; of breathing, in and out; of an understanding of the form through which the breath has to flow, prepared by a proper position of the larynx, the tongue, the nose, and the palate. Of a knowledge and understanding of the functions of the muscles of the abdomen and diaphragm, which regulate the breath pressure; then, of the chest-muscle tension, against which the breath is forced, and whence, under the control of the singer, after passing through the vocal cords, it, in a roundabout way, beats against the resonating surfaces and vibrates in the cavities of the head. Of a highly cultivated skill and flexibility in adjusting all the vocal organs and in putting them into minutely graduated movements, without inducing changes through the pronunciation of words or the execution of musical figures that shall be injurious to the tonal beauty or the artistic expression of the song. Of an immense muscular power in the breathing apparatus and all the vocal organs, the strengthening of which to endure sustained exertion cannot be begun too long in advance; and the exercising of which, as long as one sings in public, must never be remitted for a single day.

As beauty and stability of tone do not depend upon excessive *pressure* of the breath, so the muscular power of the organs used in singing does not depend on convulsive rigidity, but in that snakelike power of contracting and loosening,[1] which a singer must consciously have under perfect control.

The study needed for this occupies an entire lifetime; not only because the singer must perfect himself more and more in the rôles of his repertory—even after he has been performing them year in and year out—but because he must continually strive for progress, setting himself tasks that require greater and greater mastery and strength, and thereby demand fresh study.

He who stands still, goes backward.

Nevertheless, there are fortunately gifted geniuses in whom are already united all the qualities needed to attain greatness and perfection, and whose circumstances in life are equally fortunate, who can reach the goal earlier, without devoting their whole lives to it. Thus, for instance, in Adelina Patti everything was united—the splendid voice, paired with great talent for singing, and the long oversight of her studies by her distinguished teacher, Strakosch. She never sang rôles that did not suit her voice; in her earlier years she sang only arias and duets or single solos, never taking part in ensembles. She never sang even her limited repertory when she was indisposed. She never attended rehearsals, but came to the theatre in the evening and sang triumphantly, without ever having seen the persons who sang and acted with her. She spared herself rehearsals which, on the day of the performance, or the day before, exhaust all singers, because of the excitement of all kinds attending them, and which contribute neither to the freshness of the voice nor to the joy of the profession.

Although she was a Spaniard by birth and an American by early adoption, she was, so to speak, the greatest Italian singer of my time. All was absolutely good, correct, and flawless, the voice like a bell that you seemed to hear long after its singing had ceased.

---

[1] In physiology when the muscles resume their normal state, they are said to be *relaxed*. But as I wish to avoid giving a false conception in our vocal sensations, I prefer to use the word "loosening."

Yet she could give no explanation of her art, and answered all her colleagues' questions concerning it with an "Ah je n'en sais rien!"

She possessed, unconsciously, as a gift of nature, a union of all those qualities that all other singers must attain and possess *consciously*. Her vocal organs stood in the most favorable relations to each other. Her talent and her remarkably trained ear maintained control over the beauty of her singing and of her voice. The fortunate circumstances of her life preserved her from all injury. The purity and flawlessness of her tone, the beautiful equalization of her whole voice, constituted the magic by which she held her listeners entranced. Moreover, she was beautiful and gracious in appearance.

The accent of great dramatic power she did not possess.

Of the Breath

THE breath becomes voice through the operation of the will, and the instrumentality of the vocal organs.

To regulate the breath, to prepare a passage of the proper form through which it shall flow, circulate, develop itself, and reach the necessary resonating chambers, must be our chief task.

How did I breathe?

Being very short of breath by nature, my mother had to keep me as a little child almost sitting upright in bed. After I had outgrown that and as a big girl could run around and play well enough, I still had much trouble with shortness of breath in the beginning of my singing lessons. For years I practised breathing exercises every day without singing, and still do so, but in another way, by continually articulating syllables on a decreasing breath, for everything that concerns breath and voice has become clear to me. Soon I had succeeded so far as to be able to hold a swelling and diminishing tone quietly from fifteen to twenty seconds.

I had learned this: to draw in the abdomen and diaphragm, raise the chest and hold the breath in it by the aid of the ribs; in letting out the breath gradually to relax the abdomen. To do everything thoroughly I doubtless exaggerated it all. But since for years I have breathed in this way almost exclusively, with the utmost care, I have naturally attained great dexterity in it; and my abdominal and chest muscles and my diaphragm have been strengthened to a remarkable degree. Yet I was not satisfied.

A horn player in Berlin with the power of holding a very long breath, once told me, in answer to a question, that he drew in his abdomen and diaphragm very strongly, but immediately relaxed his abdomen again as soon as he began to play. I tried the same thing with the *best results*. Very naïve was the answer I once got from three German orchestral horn players in America. They looked at me in entire bewilderment, and

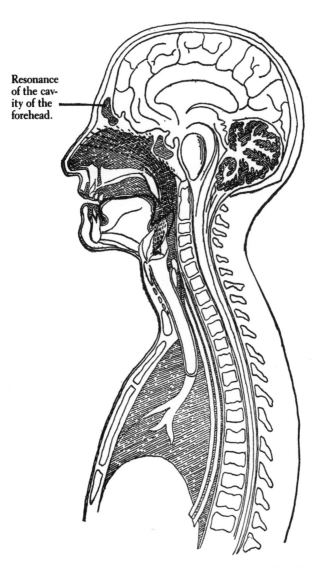

Resonance of the cavity of the forehead.

Heavy black and dotted lines denote division of the breath in the resonance of the head cavities, high range.

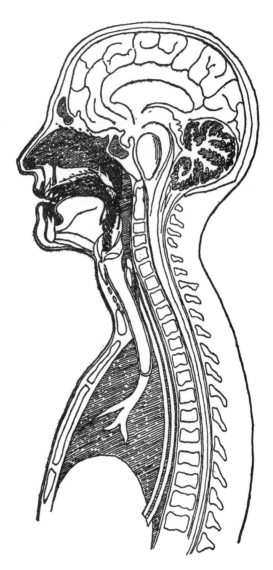

Dotted lines denote division of the breath in the middle range.

appeared not to understand in the least my questions as to how they breathed. Two of them declared that the best way was not to think about it at all. But when I asked if their teachers had never told them how they should breathe, the third answered, after some reflection, "Oh, yes!" and pointed in a general way to his stomach. The first two were right, in so far as violent inhalation of breath is really undesirable, because thereby *too much* air is drawn in. But such ignorance of the subject is disheartening, and speaks ill for the conservatories in which the players were trained, whose performances naturally are likely to give art a black eye.

Undoubtedly I took in too much air in breathing, cramped various muscles, thereby depriving my breathing organs and muscles of their elasticity. I often had, with all care and preparation for inhalation, too little breath, and sometimes, when not giving special thought to it, more than enough. I felt, too, after excessive inhalation as if I must emit a certain amount of air before I began to sing. Finally, I abandoned all superfluous drawing in of the abdomen and diaphragm, inhaled but little, and began to pay special attention to emitting the smallest possible amount of breath, which I found very serviceable.

I draw in the diaphragm and my abdomen just a little, only to relax it immediately. I raise the chest, distend the upper ribs, and support them with the lower ones like pillars under them. In this manner I prepare the form for my singing, the supply chamber for the breath, exactly as I had learned it from my mother. At the same time I raise my palate high toward the nose and prevent the escape of breath through the nose. The diaphragm beneath reacts elastically against it, and furnishes pressure from the abdomen. Chest, diaphragm, and the closed epiglottis form a supply chamber for the breath.

Only when I have begun to sing and articulate an $\bar{a}$ do I push the breath against the chest, thereby setting the chest muscles in action. These combined with the elastically stretched diaphragm and abdominal muscles—the abdomen is always brought back to its natural position during singing—exert a pressure in the form, which, as we have already learned, is the supply chamber and bed of the breath. This pressure enables us to control the breath while singing.

From this supply chamber the breath must very sparingly and gently pass far back between the vocal cords, which regulate it, and through the epiglottis. The vowel $\bar{a}$ lifts the epiglottis; it must always be kept in mind, always be placed and pronounced anew—even when other vowels are to be articulated. Then the singer only experiences the sensation of the inflated, well-closed form of the supply chamber which he must be heedful, especially when carefully articulating the consonants, not to

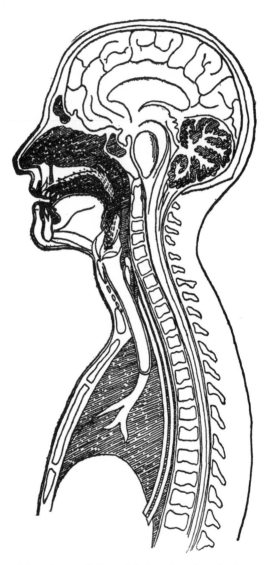

Dotted lines denote division of the breath in the palatal resonance:
lower range of male and female voices.

impair. The longer the form remains unimpaired, the less breath escapes, and the longer it may flow from the form.

This form or supply chamber, the breath pressure, which includes abdomen, diaphragm, and chest muscles, is often named "Atemstauen" (breath restraint), and "Stauprinzip" (law or principle of restraint), terms which carry in themselves the danger of inducing the pupil to make the diaphragm rigid, to hold back the breath, and to stiffen the entire vocal organs instead of making him realize that only from an eternally alive form with elastic muscular action can the breath flow, the tone resonate.

The more flexibly the breath pressure is exerted against the chest—one has the feeling in this of singing the tone against the chest from whence it must be gently and flexibly pushed out—the less the breath flows through the vocal cords and the less, consequently, are they directly burdened. The strong coöperation of chest muscles and diaphragmatic pressure prevents the overburdening of all the directly participating vocal organs.

In this way, under control, the breath reaches the tone form prepared above by the tongue; it reaches the resonance chambers prepared for it by the raising and lowering of the soft palate and those in the head cavities. Here it forms whirling currents of tone, which now fill all attainable resonating cavities necessary for tone perfection. Not until the last note of a phrase has passed the "bell" or cup-shaped cavity of mouth and lips may the breath be allowed to flow unimpeded, may the form or supply chamber be relaxed, which, nevertheless, must quickly prepare itself for the next phrase.

To observe and keep under control these many functions, singly or in conjunction, forms the ceaseless delight of the never failing fountain of song study.

In preparing the form for the flow of breath (tone flow), all the organs, abdomen, diaphragm, upper ribs, larynx, tongue, palate, nose, lungs, bronchial tubes, abdominal and chest cavities, and their muscles, participate. These organs can, to a certain degree, be relatively placed at will, and we singers are in duty bound to acquire the necessary technical skill to perform any task as nearly perfectly as possible. The vocal cords, which we can best imagine as inner lips, we do not feel. We first become conscious of them through the controlling apparatus of the breath, which teaches us to spare them, by emitting breath through them in the least possible quantity and of even pressure, thereby producing a steady tone. I even maintain that all is won if we regard them directly as breath regulators, and relieve them of all overwork through the controlling apparatus of the chest-muscle tension. With the tongue, whose back becomes our breath and pitch rudder, we are enabled to direct the breath to those resonance surfaces which are necessary for the pitch of every tone. This rule remains the same for all voices.

If for the breath there is created in the mouth an elastic form, in back of which the currents may circulate unhindered by any pressure or undue contraction or expansion, it becomes practically unlimited. That is the simple solution of the paradox that without taking a deep breath one may often have very much breath, and often after elaborate preparations none at all. Generally the chief attention is directed to inhalation, instead of to the elastic forming and agility of the organs for the breath and the minimal exhalation.

It is due only to the ignorance of the causes, to the absence of the form, to the pressure and to the convulsive tightening of the muscles, that the singer is unable to sing in one breath all that is included in the musical or speech phrase.

As soon as the breath leaves the larynx, it is divided. One part may press toward the palate, the other toward the cavities of the head. The division of the breath occurs regularly, from the deepest bass to the highest tenor or soprano, step for step, vibration for vibration, without regard to sex or individuality. Only the differing size or strength of the vocal organs through which the breath flows, the breathing apparatus, or the skill with which they are used, are different in different individuals. The seat of the breath, the law of its division, as well as the resonating surfaces, are always the same, and are differentiated at most through difference of habit.

Of the Breath and Whirling Currents
(Singing Forward)

VERY few singers know that in order to use the breath to the fullest advantage it must also remain very long diffused back in the mouth. A mistaken idea of singing forward tempts most to expel it upward with the diaphragm alone, and thus waste it—one of the most common errors. The diaphragm, to the contrary, must be relaxed after every attack—that is, it must be made pliable—an act which results in the flexibility of all muscular tension of the vocal organs. These, as soon as they are well placed (in good relation, one to the other), and tensed, will be put in an elastic condition through the gentle relaxation of the diaphragm after the attack has commanded entire energetic concentration. Naturally neither the form nor the coöperating muscular tension should be altered by it. These should only be made elastic and mobile for further demands to be put upon them. In this way the breath can be regulated and be made use of most sparingly.

The column of breath coming in an uninterrupted stream from the larynx must, as soon as it flows into the form prepared for it according to the required tone by the tongue and palate, fill this form, soaring through all its corners with its vibrations. It makes whirling currents, which circulate in the elastic form surrounding it, and it must remain there till the tone is high enough, strong enough, and sustained enough to satisfy the judgment of the singer as well as the ear of the listener. Should there be lacking the least element of pitch, strength, or duration, the tone is imperfect and does not meet the requirement.

Learning and teaching to hear is the first task of both pupil and teacher. One is impossible without the other. It is the most difficult as well as the most grateful task, and it is the only way to reach perfection.

Even if the pupil unconsciously should produce a flawless tone, it is the teacher's duty to acquaint him clearly with the *causes* of it. It is not

15

enough to sing well; one must also know how one does it. The teacher must examine the pupil constantly, making him describe clearly his sensations in singing, and understand fully the physiological factors that coöperate to produce them.

The sensations in singing must coincide with the ones here described, if they are to be considered as correct; for mine are based logically on physiological causes, and correspond precisely with the operation of these causes. Moreover, all my pupils tell me—often, to be sure, not till many months have passed—how exact my explanations are; how accurately, on the strength of them, they have learned to feel the physiological processes. They have learned, slowly, to be sure, to become conscious of their errors and false impressions; for it is very difficult to ascertain such mistakes and false adjustments of the organs. False sensations in singing, and disregarded or false ideas of physiological processes cannot immediately be stamped out. A long time is needed for the mind to be able to form a clear image of those processes, and not till then can knowledge and improvement be expected. The teacher must repeatedly explain the physiological processes, the pupil repeatedly disclose every confusion and uncertainty he feels, until the perfect consciousness of his sensations in singing is irrevocably impressed upon his memory, that is, has become a habit.

Among a hundred singers hardly one can be found whose single tones meet every requirement.

I admit that such perfect tones sometimes, generally quite unconsciously, are heard from young singers, and especially from beginners, and never fail to make an impression. The teacher hears that they are good, so does the public. Only a very few, even among singers, know why, because only a very few know the laws governing perfect tone production. Their talent, their ear perchance, tell them the truth; but the causes they neither know nor look for.

I shall be told that tones well sung, even unconsciously, are enough. But that is not true. The least unfavorable circumstance, over-exertion, indisposition, an unaccustomed situation, anything can blow out the "unconscious" one's light, or at least make it flicker badly. Of any self-help, when there is ignorance of all the fundamentals, there can be no question. Any help is grasped at.

This is not remarkable, in view of the complexity of the phenomena of song. Few teachers concern themselves with the fundamental studies; they often do not sing at all, or they sing quite wrongly; and consequently can neither describe the vocal sensations nor test them in others. Theory alone is of no value whatever.

The Singer's Physiological Studies

SCIENCE has explained all the processes of the vocal organs in their chief functions, and many methods of singing have been based upon physiology, physics, and phonetics. To a certain extent scientific explanations are absolutely necessary to the singer—as long as they are confined to the sensations in singing, foster understanding of the phenomenon, and summon an intelligible picture for the hitherto unexplained voice-sensations, or for the ordinarily misunderstood expressions of "full," "bright," "dark," "nasal," "singing forward," etc. They are quite meaningless without the practical teachings of the sensations of such singers as have directed their attention to them with a knowledge of the end in view, and are competent to correlate them with the facts of science.

The singer is usually worried by the word "physiology," but only because he does not clearly understand how to limit his knowledge of it. But he ought to, and should want to know the little that is necessary. It means that the muscles of the nose, which inflate the nostrils, place the soft palate high or flatly downward; that they also influence the pillars of the fauces by letting them, at different stages, draw themselves like a saddle upward toward the nose. It means that the tongue is able to take many different positions, and that the larynx with the help of $\overline{oo}$ takes a low position and with the vowels $\bar{a}$ and $\bar{e}$ a high one, closer to the palate. It means that all muscles contract during activity and relax during normal inactivity; that they must be strengthened by continued vocal gymnastics so that they may be able to sustain long and continued exertion, and retain their elasticity, and operate elastically. Furthermore, it means the exact knowledge of the activity of diaphragm, chest, throat and facial muscles.

This is all that physiology means for the vocal organs. Since these things all operate together, one without the others can accomplish nothing; if the least is lacking, singing is quite impossible, or is entirely bad.

17

Physiology is concerned also with muscles, nerves, sinews, ligaments, and cartilage, all of which are used in singing, but all of which we cannot feel. We cannot even feel the vocal cords. Certainly much depends for the singer upon their proper condition; and whether as voice producers or breath regulators, we all have good reason to spare them always as much as possible, and never to overburden them.

Though we cannot feel the vocal cords, we can, nevertheless, hear, by observing whether the tone is even—in the emission of the breath under control—whether they are performing their functions properly. Overburdening them through the pressure of uncontrolled breath results in complete vocal languor. The irritation of severe coughing, thoughtless talking, or shouting immediately after singing may also set up serious congestion of the vocal cords, which can be remedied only through slow gymnastics of the tongue and laryngeal muscles, by the pronunciation of vowels in conjunction with consonants. Inactivity of the vocal organs will not cure it, or perhaps not till after the lapse of years. (See exercise yā, yē, yōō, yäh, yü.)

A good singer can *never* lose his voice. Mental agitation or severe colds can for a time deprive the singer of the use of his vocal organs, or seriously impair them. Only those who have been singing without consciously correct use of their organs can become disheartened over it; those who know better will, with more or less difficulty, cure themselves, and by the use of vocal gymnastics bring their vocal organs into condition again.

For this reason, if for no other, singers should seek to acquire accurate knowledge of their own organs, as well as of their functions, that they may not let themselves be burnt, cut, and cauterized by unscrupulous physicians. Leave the larynx and all connected with it alone; strengthen the organs by daily vocal gymnastics and a healthy, *sober* mode of life; beware of catching cold after singing; do not sit and talk in restaurants.

Students of singing should use the early morning hours, and fill their days with the various branches of their study. Sing every day only so much, that on the next day you can practise again, feeling fresh and ready for work, as *regular* study requires. Better one hour every day than ten to-day and none to-morrow.

The public singer should also do his practising early in the day, that he may have himself well in hand by evening. How often one feels indisposed in the morning! Any physical reason is sufficient to make singing difficult, or even impossible; it need not be connected necessarily with the vocal organs; in fact, I believe it very rarely is. For this reason, in two hours everything may have changed.

I remember a charming incident in New York. Albert Niemann, our

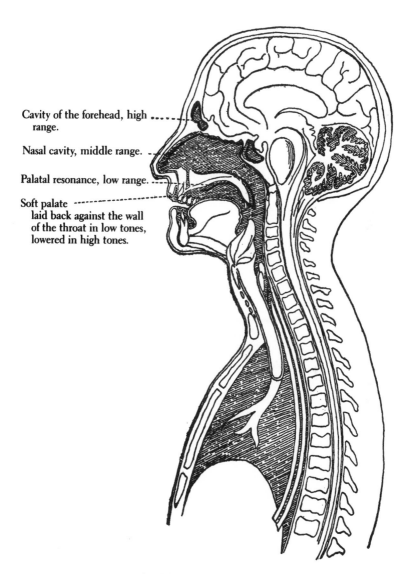

Cavity of the forehead, high range.

Nasal cavity, middle range.

Palatal resonance, low range.

Soft palate laid back against the wall of the throat in low tones, lowered in high tones.

Heavy black lines denote the resonance.

heroic tenor, who was to sing *Lohengrin* in the evening, complained to me in the morning of severe hoarseness. To give up a rôle in America costs the singer, as well as the director, much money. My advice was to wait.

Niemann. What do you do, then, when you are hoarse?

I. Oh, I practise and see whether I cannot sing in spite of it.

Niem. Indeed; and what do you practise?

I. Long, slow scales.

Niem. Even if you are hoarse?

I. Yes; if I want to sing, or have to, I try it.

Niem. Well, what are they? Show me.

The great scale, the infallible cure. (See page 96.)

I showed them to him; he sang them, with words of abuse in the meantime; but gradually his hoarseness grew better. He did not send word of his inability to appear in the evening, but sang, and better than ever, with enormous success.

I myself had to sing *Norma* in Vienna some years ago, and got up in the morning quite hoarse. By nine o'clock I tried my infallible remedy, but could not sing above A flat, though in the evening I should have to reach high D flat and E flat. I was on the point of giving up, because the case seemed to me so desperate. Nevertheless, I practised till eleven o'clock, half an hour at a time, and noticed that I was gradually getting better. In the evening I had my D flat and E flat at my command and was in brilliant form. People said they had seldom heard me sing so well.

I could give numberless instances, all going to show that you never can tell early in the day how you are going to feel in the evening. I much prefer, for instance, not to feel so very well early in the day, because it may easily happen that the opposite will be the case later on, which is much less agreeable. If you wish to sing only when you are in good form, you must excuse yourself ninety-nine times out of a hundred. You must learn to know your own vocal organs thoroughly and be able to sing; must do everything that is calculated to keep you in good condition. This includes chiefly rest for the nerves, care of the body, and gymnastics of the voice, that you may be able to defy all possible chances.

Before all, never neglect to practise every morning, regularly, proper singing exercises through the whole compass of the voice. Do it with *painful* seriousness; and never think that vocal gymnastics weary the singer. On the contrary, they bring refreshment and power of endurance to him who will become master of his vocal organs. This is the duty of every singer who wants to exercise his art publicly.

Equalizing the Voice—Form

IN the lowest range of female and male voices—with the latter it occurs in nearly the entire compass of the voice—the passage to the resonance of the head cavities is well-nigh cut off, the pillars of the fauces being stretched over the pharynx and drawn back to the wall of the throat, thus confining tonal sound almost exclusively to palatal and chest resonance. The larynx is to be thought of as being placed flexibly against the palate. The tension between $\bar{e}$, $\bar{a}$, $\overline{oo}$ is very little, rather horizontal than perpendicular; the vocal cords are tensed but little. The covering for the tone created by the $\overline{oo}$ is felt in velvetlike softness at the nose and, while singing, like a big arch extending along the palate toward the back. It is united to all other vowels and organs by means of y. This we call the chest voice, the most powerful of all ranges. (From the gramophone reproductions, you can distinctly hear how much more sonorous the voices of men who sing exclusively with chest voice sound than those of the female, whose chest notes are the exception.)

By raising the soft palate—peak—behind the nose (sensation is like a mild elastic cold in the nose), raising the back of the tongue, placing the larynx closer by means of $\bar{a}$, and by tensing the vocal cords by means of $\bar{e}$ upward and $\overline{oo}$ downward the pillars of the fauces are drawn together, thus freeing a passage for the breath or tone toward the head cavities, the resonance of which it now puts to good account. This is the head tone, the highest range of all voices, the falsetto—the thinnest range, whose characteristic quality, however, is the greatest degree of carrying power.

Between these two extreme functions of the vocal organs, the deepest chest and the highest purest head voice or falsetto, lie all grades of the lower and higher middle range, as well as the mixed chest and head voice, the "voix mixte," everything which may be secured through the adjustment of the muscles of the vocal organs, that is, through the fit adjustment of the vocal organs in vowel mixing. (See plates.)

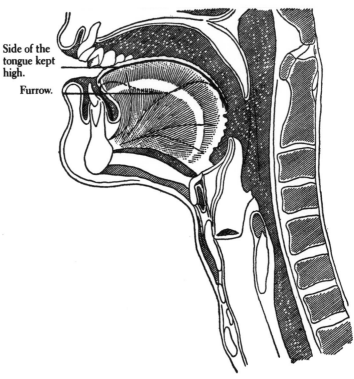

Side of the
tongue kept
high.

Furrow.

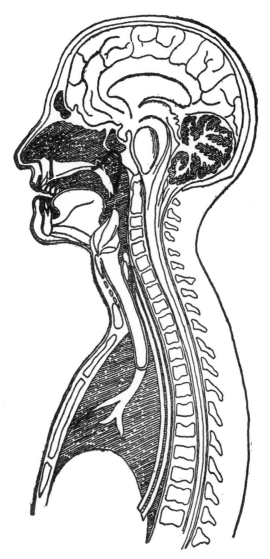

Heavy black line denotes sensation for the propagation form.

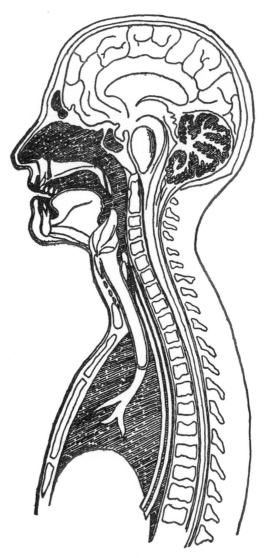

Heavy black line denotes:
Sensation in raising the soft palate for high notes.
Sensation of the form in rapid upward passages.
Division of the breath favors the resonance of head cavities.

The palatal sensation which is here indicated by black lines is naturally only a sensation. It is accounted for in the tension of another muscle that begins above the palate, divides in two parts, and extends along and down the back of the throat. It is a stretching muscle which, as soon as the pillars of the fauces are raised, puts in its appearance and creates the sensation as if the pillars of the fauces extended in a wide curve directly from the nose down to the diaphragm. As a matter of fact the pillars of the fauces draw more and more together toward the top the higher we ascend with the tones. The sensation, however, increases through this counter-tension downward.

If I said in the foregoing that in the case of the chest voice the passage to the head voice is almost cut off by the stretching of the pillars of the

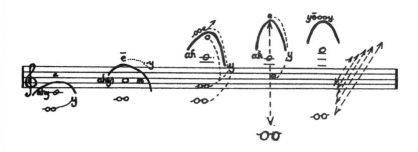

fauces over the throat, a branch stream of breath, however small, must penetrate behind and above the pillars, with *ē* at the nose, and later to the forehead and head cavities. This creates overtones (head tones) which must vibrate in all tones, even in the lowest. These overtones lead from

the purest chest tones, slowly, with a constantly changing mixture of both kinds of resonance, first to the high tones of bass and baritone, the low tones of tenor, the middle tones of alto and soprano, finally to the purest head tones, the highest tones of the tenor (falsetto), or soprano. (See the plates.)

The extremely delicate gradation of the scale of increase to the resonance of the head cavities in ascending passages, and of increase of palatal resonance in descending, depends upon the skill to make the palate, tongue, and larynx act elastically and to let the breath, continually controlled by relaxing the abdominal pressure and the narrow placement of the chest pressure, flow uninterruptedly in a gentle stream into the closely connected resonating chambers. Through the previous preparation of the larynx and tongue, it must reach its resonating surfaces as though passing through a cylinder, and must circulate in the form previously prepared for it, proper for each tone and vowel sound. This form surrounds it gently but firmly. The supply of air remains continuously the same, *rather increasing than diminishing,* notwithstanding the fact that the quantity which the abdominal pressure has furnished the vocal cords from the supply chamber is a very small one. That it may not hinder further progression, the form must remain elastic and sensitive to the most delicate modification of the vowel sound. If the tone is to have life, it must always be able to conform to any vowel sound. The least displacement of the form through laxness of articulation or laxness of muscle tension breaks up the whirling currents and vibrations, and consequently affects the tone, its vibrancy, its strength and its duration.

In singing a continuous passage upward the form becomes higher by means of *ē* and more pliant by means of *o͞o*; the most pliable place on the palate is drawn upward.

When I sing a single tone I can give it much more power, and much more palatal, chest, or nasal resonance, than I could give in a series of ascending tones. In a musical figure I *must place the lowest note in such a way that I can easily reach the highest*. I must, therefore, give it much more head tone than the single tone requires. (Very important.) When advancing farther, I have the feeling on the palate, above and behind the nose, toward the cavities of the head, of a strong but very elastic rubber ball, which I fill like a balloon with my breath streaming up far back of it. And this filling keeps on in even measure. That is, the branch stream of breath, which, coming from the chest in whirling currents, penetrates the head cavities, must be free to flow unhindered from the mouth after the work with *ē* has been completed.

I can increase the size of this ball above to a pear shape, as soon as I think of singing higher; and, indeed, I heighten the form by making it supple before I go on from the tone just sung, placing it, so to speak, higher, and keep in this way the form, that is, the "propagation form," ready for the next higher tone, which I can now reach easily as long as no interruption in the stream of breath against the mucous membrane can take place. For this reason the upward-flowing breath in back must never be pressed but must always flow. The higher the tone, the more numerous are the vibrations, the more rapidly the whirling currents circulate, and the more one has the sensation of a perpendicular tone or breath form. Catarrh often dries up the mucous membrane; then the tones are inclined to break off. At such times one must sing with peculiar circumspection, and with an especially powerful stream of breath behind the tone: it is better to take breath frequently. In a descending scale or figure I must, on the contrary, preserve very carefully the form taken for the highest tone, must think it higher, under no circumstances lower, but must apparently keep the same height and imagine that I am striking the same tone again. The form may gradually be a little modified at the upper end; this is, the soft palate is lowered very carefully toward the nose: keeping almost always to the form employed for the highest tone, sing the figure to its end, toward the nose, with the help of the vowel *oo*. This auxiliary vowel *oo* means nothing more than that the larynx is slowly lowered in position, which act must be renewed at every change of tone or letter.

When this happens, the resonance of the head cavities is diminished, that of the palate, and little by little that of the chest, increased; for the soft palate sinks, and the pillars of the fauces are inflated more and more. Yet the head tone must not be entirely free from palatal resonance. Both remain to the last breath united, mutually supporting each other in ascending and descending passages, and alternately but inaudibly increasing and diminishing. These things go to make up the form: the tensing of the nose, the raising and lowering of the soft palate, and the corresponding raising and lowering of the pillars of the fauces, the gentle downward relaxation of the chin. It is drawn very far backward so that the tongue stands high out of the throat and that the larynx may move freely under the tongue.

The proper position of the tongue: the tip rests on the lower front teeth—mine even as low as the roots of the teeth.

The back of the tongue must stand high and free from the throat, ready for any movement. *A furrow must be formed in the tongue*, which is least prominent in the lowest tones, and in direct head tones may even completely disappear. As soon as the tone demands the palatal resonance, the furrow must be made prominent and kept so. In my case it can always be seen, when I do not want to sing particularly dark, that is, cover the tone. This is one of the most important matters upon which too much emphasis can hardly be laid. As soon as the furrow in the tongue shows itself, the mass of the tongue is kept away from the throat since the sides are raised. Then the tone must sound right. Still there are singers whose tongues lie very well without a furrow.

It lies flattest in the lowest tones because the larynx then is in a very horizontal position, and thus is out of its way.

Furthermore, there is the unconstrained position of the larynx, which must operate without pressure of tongue and root of tongue. From it the breath must stream forth evenly and uninterruptedly, to fill the form prepared for it by the tongue and palate and supported by the throat muscles.

This support must not, however, depend in the least upon *pressure*, but upon the greatest elastic tension. One must play with the muscles, and be able to contract and relax them at pleasure, having thus perfect mastery over them. For this incessant practice is required, ceaseless control of the form through the sense of hearing, the breath pressure, and the constant articulation of certain vowels.

At first a very strong will power is needed to hold the muscles tense without pressure, that is, to let the tone soar, as it were, through the throat, mouth, or cavities of the head.

The stronger the improper pressure in the production of the tone, the more difficult it is to get rid of. The result is simply, in other words, a strain. The contraction of the muscles must go only so far that they can be slowly relaxed; that is, can return to their normal position *easily*. Never must the neck be swelled up, or the veins in it stand out. *Every convulsive or painful feeling is wrong.*

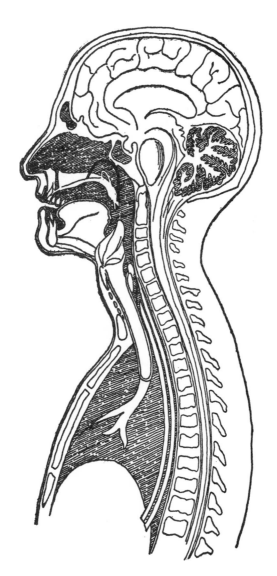

Heavy black line denotes sensation of the form in slow progression of tones.

The Attack and the Vowels

OUR ear perceives sounds. A single tone as ordinarily held in the conception of singer and listener does not really exist. To the musician each separate tone holds component parts that give height, strength, and depth. As soon as the singer realizes this very important point, he will comprehend the difficulties of the vocal art and will learn to overcome them.

The Attack

In the attack the breath must be directed to a focal point on the palate which lies under the tone-height. And now, uniting with it strength and depth, it is made to resonate in this strongly concentrated space formed by the relative position of the vocal organs.

To this end are necessary a knowledge of all vowel functions and a well-trained ear sensitive to all perfect vowels used in singing; not those that have become habit through the uncontrolled speech of the untrained but those which the noble art of song demands.

Often great misunderstandings, if not, indeed, ill effects, are brought about when teachers in the beginning of their instruction demand of their pupils pure-sounding vowels, for pure vowels in the strict sense of tonal art cannot—unless the pupil is unusually favored—be produced at all.

The pure singing or tone vowel is not at all pure in the ordinary sense of the word. On the contrary, because of the tone-form necessary, it is rather complicated. It even becomes more complicated through the different tone colorings which it is compelled to adopt according to register, pitch, interval, syllable, and word combination, usage of speech, or tonal art. It is possible to sing twenty different $\bar{e}$, $\bar{a}$, ah, $\bar{o}$, $\overline{oo}$'s which in their own nature, already mixed, sound pure and intelligible in the word. The vocal organs must adjust themselves simultaneously to the speech usage and art of song to aid one in striving toward the highest degree of beauty and ability.

The teacher must, while the pupils sing, begin to explain the tone form, how the vowel is really made with the aid of other vowels; and draw their attention to the coöperation of the different vowels on each tone while they are vocalizing. They must learn to unite one vowel with another by the aid of the semi-vowel *y*. Then they must be taught to combine two and three and gradually be made to enunciate them artistically. A perfect tone can only be made by the skilful blending of several vowels; and on the other hand well-sounding vowels of carrying quality can only be created in a perfect tone. In the recognition of the complicated process of uniting several vowel forms to make one lies the secret of the true attack, the foundation pile and conception of which we are now ready to consider.

If one has tabulated the vowels for the physiological processes of the vocal organs, and accustomed oneself to think in these vowels musically, it is not difficult to set the correct form for the attack, provided one has through practice fully mastered the work of each separate vowel.

Above all strike out the so-called pure vowel *ah*—since it is the root of all evil—and also eliminate from the memory that it is a single tone. Even though the vowel *ah* in various combinations sounds like *ah*, it has, notwithstanding its fundamental feature of vowel blending necessary to its tone form, nothing in common with the accustomed vowel *ah* as it is ordinarily spoken. Our musical table for the vowel *ah* and for the attack presents itself as follows:

Vowel *ē*=tone-height, tone-carrier, head voice.

  ā=strength, brightness, place determining vowel, note line upon which we sing.

  ōō=tone-depth, flexibility, covering, euphony, chest resonance.

These three vowels, concentrated in the proper mixture and attacked simultaneously, give the vowel *ah* as the artist needs it. They determine the fundamental position of each tone, and are at the same time the attack itself, which is neither a single vowel nor a separate function of the vocal organs but a triple sound on one tone.

As here three vowels flow together, which we must according to necessity change and yet unite, we still need another binding medium by which the closed form will be kept flexible. For this purpose we can best use the semi-vowel *y*. It is pronounced with the broad back of the tongue against the soft palate which sinks toward the tongue and thus closes off the form of the inner mouth. If we do not wholly dissolve the *y* position

while pronouncing vowels, consonants, and words, that is, if we do not
entirely remove the back of the tongue from the soft palate, and if in
addition pronounce or think $\overline{oo}$ thereto, then the middle part of the tongue
falls under the teeth, the soft palate draws upward toward the nose and the
vowel form remains prepared for each succeeding vowel. It is best to
imagine the *y* as a hinge formed with tongue and palate. It binds all letters
with one another. Shut in the back by the union of palate and back of
tongue and also the pillars of the fauces, it allows of a flexible opening
upward toward the nose by means of *ē* and downward toward the chin by
means of $\overline{oo}$. The *ē* and $\overline{oo}$, though, are fastened to the hinge as if by
rubber bands.

The ordinary *ah*, as practically pronounced by every layman, and so
often demanded by many teachers of their pupils, is an absurdity, as the
tongue is usually pressed down—
not only by false habit but often
pressed down artificially with
instruments. This leads to flat, ordi-
nary, defective singing, if not often to the ruin of the voice itself, *e.g.*
begin to pronounce from *y*.

In pronouncing the vowel *ē* all the tendons and muscles of the nose
and cheeks are drawn into activity. The nostrils and with them the pillars
of the fauces distend.

With *ā* we place the larynx closer under the nose and connect both
vowels so that when we say *ā* we mix it with *ē* and when we say *ē* we mix
it energetically with *ā*.

The *ā* position is the first and chief action for the attack for all singing
and pronunciation and must under all conditions—whether narrower or
wider, darker or brighter, stronger or entirely toned down—be always
retained because through this position, only, the breath finds its attack on
the hard palate. The *ā* gives the tone concentrated strength; it opens the
epiglottis. It frequently happens that pupils, even singers, do not set the
larynx in place at all; the tone lacks strength and energy and wavers to and
fro without support. Such a fault can only be remedied if the pupil or
singer energetically sets *ā* before every tone or letter, in doing which he
must have the sensation of pushing the larynx directly under the nose into
the chin.

After having secured the first position setting the larynx with *ā*, we,
with our thoughts dwelling on *ē*, place the broad back of the flexible
tongue against the entire palate which sinks toward it. The nose dilates
still wider and we reach—as if drawn by rubber bands—the *ē* which
vibrates above the nose, by which action the larynx fixes itself still closer,

that is, it raises itself in the back a little toward $\bar{e}$ through the position of the tongue, and places itself downward in front with $\bar{a}$ pushed somewhat before the $\overline{oo}$. Avoid all pressure of the tongue! From this second position we pass to the third as soon as we have assured ourselves of the y hinge. With our thoughts on $\overline{oo}$ we then draw back quickly the point of the tongue from under the lower teeth and let everything that lies under the tongue drop flexibly and pronounce now, with the lips pushed forward, the vowel $\overline{oo}$. By means of y, $\bar{a}$ remains joined to $\bar{e}$ and cannot and must not be lost in any vowel. Through this tongue and larynx action the soft palate has separated itself from the back of the tongue, leans toward the nose, and so covers the tone. But the back of the tongue nevertheless lies in the y position as high and supple as possible. By means of the tongue thus raised, the closely but flexibly held larynx, and the free and slightly covered nose, the two bright vowels partially remain, and combine with them the dark vowel, thus making a complete singing tone—that is, the requisite triple-vowel sound with sounds like ah which isn't it in the usual comprehension. In the gently concentrated $\bar{a}$- and $\bar{e}$- form a minute space between the fore part of the tongue and the palate is created by the above-mentioned change, a space which gives place to the tone that is now mixed with chest resonance. By setting the larynx low, or, better, by making it supple, the chest resonance is introduced. By means of the y-form, which is closed toward the back of the mouth, the tone is kept forward; and this kind of singing—there is only one really good kind, which varies in each individual according to the size of the voice and the skill—is called singing toward the front.

The sensation created by the relative position of the triple-vowel sound stretches from the nose over the palate, over the back and root of tongue, larynx, chest, ribs, down to the diaphragm. The higher we wish to sing, the more positive and elastic we have to regard the $\bar{a}$-line as the centre of each tone and attack. The higher and more flexibly the nose and tongue function with $\bar{e}$ and $\bar{a}$, so much deeper down to the diaphragm the tension with $\overline{oo}$ extends, which then seems to ring out in $\bar{e}$ and beyond it, as if it were a perpendicularly stretched string. Cramp or pressure is not allowable, but a very strong energy is necessary to preserve the muscular tension—in spite of its firmness—elastic, well-balanced, and still keep united the various muscles put in play.

With the vowel ah we must especially see that the tongue, accustomed to wrong usage, under no condition returns to its old position but that it is always directed by y to its true position. If in the beginning the vowel ah created on the triple-vowel basis sounds at times more like $\bar{a}$ or $\bar{e}$ or $\overline{oo}$, we must not become disconcerted, for through conscious practice the tongue will, notwithstanding, become accustomed to its work. There is no other road to perfection.

If the difficulties of the *ah* lie in the giving up of old habits and in the readjustment on the triple-vowel basis, then the *ā* vowel brings others with it. As I have said before in speaking of the attack, in order to make the vowel-sound *ā*, the larnyx is with energy brought in closer relation with the nose. By dilating the nostrils a preparation is made. The sensation is then as if the larynx were under the nose in the chin. If we then sing *ā* energetically we soon become conscious of an inherent strength which is created partially by the energetic opening of the epiglottis in the pronunciation of *ā* and partially by the position of the larynx which makes possible the attack of the breath on the hard palate. This *ā-* strength must be inherent in every tone, indeed in every letter. Wisely to use it, to distribute it, apply it flexibly, not to overstrain it in the *fortissimo* nor lose it in the *piano* is an art in itself, and, moreover, a great part of the art of singing.

For me *ā* is the note-line on which, as on a balance, I measure my tone power, weighing it as if on a scale, balancing it upward and downward. It is the kernel of every tone, the binding medium between strong and weak. It is a power that we must continually economize and yet again lavishly but wisely expend.

So many singers are, for this reason, not able to "markier" (to outline a composition by accenting certain notes) because they let go of this elastic but energetic strength of the *ā*-position, and have nothing left but a disunited *ē*, unsupported by *ā*, which suffices for the loose head tones of the higher range but is inadequate when the singer wishes to "markier" in a lower range. To markier does not mean to destroy the relative position of the vocal organs, nor to relax the muscular tension and only to peep, but to sing easily and well with the completely established relation of the vocal organs—whose power only is diminished. (See section on Markieren in chapter "My Own Practice in Singing.")

We must therefore in the softest *piano* make use of this power necessary to the perfect tone, and keep it flexible with energy. We may distribute it elastically, we may increase it, by extending it to the helping vowels and organs, we may decrease it to its minimum power, but never wholly dispense with it.

It transfers itself into energy, which, swayed on elastic foundation, supported by elastic muscles of the vocal organs, must ever be present; even, then, when we are not singing, that is, during the pauses in a song or rôle. This energy which has during the pauses readjusted itself in preparatory concentration, must exist continuously in our body, and it

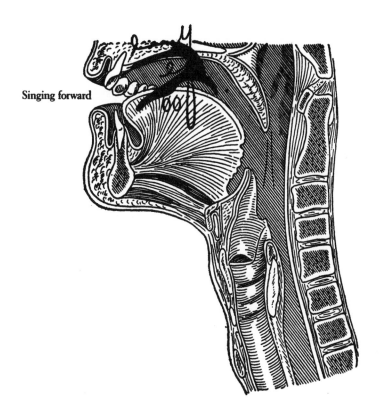

Singing forward

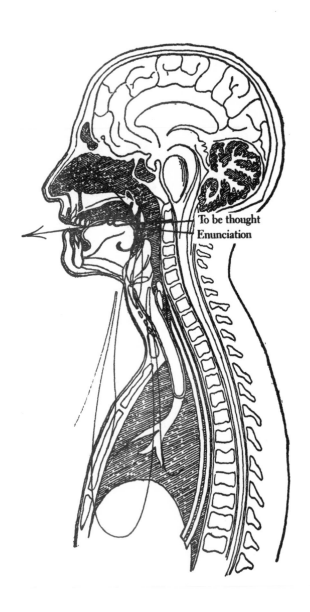

To be thought
Enunciation

must impart itself to the listener (who is unconscious of its effect)—and be a binding link between artist and audience.

Our brightest vowel $\bar{e}$ would be weak and colorless without the help of $\bar{a}$. Both vowels are closely united and are dependent on each other; $\bar{e}$ receives strength from $\bar{a}$; $\bar{a}$, lightness and tone-height from $\bar{e}$. Think them united at the nose as if with a rubber band. In continual change, closely united, they meet first at one and then at another end of their course. Neither must $\overline{oo}$ ever be sung or spoken alone. It retains the $\bar{a}$ position,

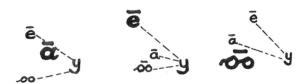

for without it it would sound hollow and weak. It always needs in addition the help of $\bar{e}$, which opens the much covered nose.

We have now sufficient proof that one vowel can never be sung alone, as tonal perfection and the art of song make other demands. Not until all vowel positions have become habit to the quickly acting memory and to the muscles, dare we speak of technical artistic skill, and are we able to rely on our knowledge. Then only can we speak of a musically trained ear, when all the demands that art has a right to exact have become clear. This is not all; in addition to the mixing of vowels, we must think of enunciating them, which is of the greatest importance to the word which is to be pronounced, and not only think of the necessary tone color for each word and letter.

The vowel o is uncomfortable, inasmuch as one is easily tempted to exaggerate the necessary enlargement of the form. We must hold the enlarged form round and cut off and make all helping vowels like $\bar{e}$, $\bar{a}$, $\overline{oo}$ still more flexible than with other letters.

In order to comprehend all of this, we must at first exaggerate everything, also the vowel-coloring. But as soon as, led by good teachers, we become sure of our ear and judgment, we begin to see how the smallest nuances change the tone and how fine the effect is. The more delicately they are applied in the various degress of strength, the richer the color, the nobler and more vital they will be able to harmonize tone, word, and sentiment which the soul of the artist desires to express.

Nasal—Nasal Singing—
Singing Toward the Nose—Covering the Tone—
Chanter dans le Masque—Nasal Twang

BY raising, rounding, and spreading the pillars of the fauces (rather far back) and jamming the broad back of the tongue against them, the "nasal" is created; with dark vowels like *ung*, *ong* to which belongs the cloudy *ang* very far back, with the brighter vowels *ing*, *eng* farther front. It is closely related to *y* and shuts off the front cavity of the mouth from the pharynx.

The nasal may be exaggerated. That always happens when the larynx does not articulate *ā* into it; the pillars of the fauces are drawn up too high, the tongue in ascending lies too flat, throat and tone open without support. This is known as open singing. It destroys the pitch, and the singer's career is doomed. To insure the form, it is constantly necessary to mix bright vowels with dark ones. The flat open *äh* must be avoided. It must always be mixed with all auxiliary vowels; it must be supplied with all connectives to the propagating form.

The nasal can be neglected, which very often happens; certain it is that it is not nearly enough used.

The Germans have only small opportunity to make the acquaintance of the nasal sound; they know it in only a few words: "E*ng*el," "la*ng*e," "Ma*ng*el," etc.,—always where *ng* occurs before or after a vowel.

The French, on the contrary, always sing and speak nasally—with the pillars of the fauces raised high, and the back of the tongue high against them—and not seldom exaggerate it. On account of the spreading of the palate, which, through the power of habit, is cultivated especially by the French to an extraordinary degree, and which affords the breath an enormous space as a resonating surface to act upon, their voices often sound tremendous. Such voices have only the one drawback, of easily becoming monotonous. At first the power of the organ astonishes us; the next time we are disappointed—the tone color remains always the same. The tone often even degenerates into a hollow quality. On the other hand, voices that are not sufficiently nasal sound colorless, clear, and expressionless.

There are singers, too, who pursue the middle path with consummate art—Meschaert, for example.

To fix the pupil's attention on the nasal tone and the elasticity of the palate, he should often be given exercises with French words.

Singing nasal or toward the nose (not to be confounded with "nasal twang," which is produced by a high larynx and by pinching the tongue on *ä*) cannot be enough studied and utilized. On account of its tonal effect, its noble timbre, it should be amply employed on all kinds of voices. By it is effected the connection of tones with each other, from the lowest chest to the highest head voice; all the beauty of the cantilena lies in the conscious application of it. This is all that singers mean when they speak of "nasal singing"—really only singing toward the nose. Palate and back of tongue, laid one toward the other, create a covering for the tone which is called "covering the tone," in French "chanter dans le masque," which, however, I mean to explain still differently.

How little the teachers speak of it is shown by the fact that many singers are quite ignorant of what nasal singing means; and when by chance they hear something about it, they are tormented by the idea of "singing toward the nose." They generally regard the voice as one complete organ acting by itself, one thing always the same. Of what can be made of it through knowledge of the functions of all the coöperating organs they know nothing.

Bass   Baritone   Tenor   Alto & Soprano

etc.

In these ranges the tone is usually covered by good artists. Yet tone covering should gradually begin in the preceding tones so that these do not suddenly sound like another register. Covering a tone draws in the assistance of the vowel $\overline{oo}$ in ascending tones. Understand me well, it draws in the assistance of other vowels as well, not $\overline{oo}$ alone; it makes the larynx more pliable, and therefore makes the ascending into a higher range easier as it directs the resonance into other forms. In male voices "tone covering" is more striking than in female voices. Yet all kinds of voices demand its utilization, if the singer wishes to lay claim to perfection and noble timbre.

Blind voices are caused by the exaggerated practice of the "nasal singing" which the singers concerned do not sufficiently diminish in the

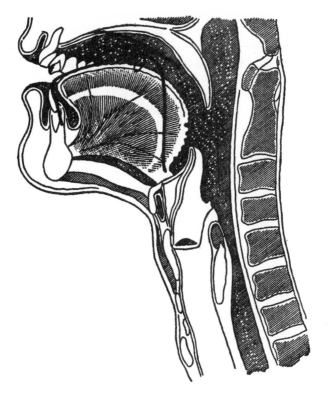

Heavy black lines denote movement of the tongue and palate
for the nasal tone.

head voice, drawing the pillars of the fauces too far toward the wall of the throat and so closing off the passage toward the head cavities.

The causes of defective tone production:

Pinched tone—$\bar{a}$ too flat and pressed.

Hollow tone—the $\overline{oo}$ too hollow—the $\bar{a}$ missing.

Too pointed tone—the $\bar{e}$ too sharp.

Flat tone—a flat and unmixed $\ddot{a}h$.

Open tone—with open throat—unmixed $\ddot{a}h$.

Throaty tone—here the tongue lies on the larynx. Bad articulation of $\bar{a}$ and $\bar{e}$.

Hard tone—cramped tension of breathing and singing muscles.

Shaky tone—tone without support. Larynx is not adjusted; it is not connected with the chest muscles.

Many singers persist in the bad habits here described as long as nature can endure it; in the course of time, however, even with the most powerful physiques, they will begin to sing noticeably flat; in the case of the less powerful, the fatal tremolo will make its appearance, which results in the ruin of so many singers.

How often have I heard young singers say, "I no longer have the power to respond to the demands made upon me," whereas the trouble lies only in the insufficient use of the resonance of the head cavities. It should never be forgotten that as the posture of the voice changes, the position of the organs cannot remain the same.

The Head Voice

THE head tone signifies youth for all voices, from the deepest bass to the highest soprano—leaving out of question the fact that it furnishes the overtones for each single tone of the whole vocal gamut. A voice without vibrancy is an *old* voice. The magic of youth, freshness, is given by the overtones that sound with every tone. Height, youth, freshness of the voice=$\bar{a}$ and $\bar{e}$.

So to utilize the head voice (resonance of the head cavities) that every tone shall be able to "carry" and shall remain high enough to reach higher tones easily, is a difficult art, without which, however, the singer cannot reckon upon the durability of his voice. Often employed unconsciously, it is lost through heedlessness, mistaken method, or ignorance; and it can hardly ever be regained, or, if at all, only through the greatest sacrifice of time, trouble, and patience.

The *pure* head voice (the third position) is, on account of the thinness that it has by nature, the neglected step-child of almost all singers, male and female; its step-parents, in the worst significance of the word, are most singing teachers, male and female. It is produced by the complete lowering of the pillars of the fauces, while the softest point of the palate—behind the nose—is thrown up very high, seemingly almost into the head, in the highest position, still higher, thinking $\bar{e}$ above the head.

The back of the tongue stands high; and the larynx also, in the sensation of it, stands high and supple under the tongue. All organs are elastic; nothing must be cramped or exaggerated.

Up to a certain pitch, with tenors as well as with sopranos, the head tones should be mixed with chest-resonance. With tenors this will be a matter of course, though with them the chest tones are much abused; with sopranos, however, a judicious mixture may be recommended because more expression is required (since the influence of Wagner has become

42

paramount in interpreting the meaning of a composition, especially of the words) than in the brilliant fireworks of former times. The head voice, too, must not be regarded as a definite register of its own. If it is suddenly heard alone—I mean disconnected with chest or palatal resonance—after forcing the preceding tones of the higher middle range, it is of course noticeably thin and stands out to its disadvantage like any sharply defined position from the middle tones. In the formation of the voice no "register" should exist or be created; the voice must be made even throughout its entire range. I do not mean by this that I should sing neither with chest tones nor with head tones. On the contrary, the practised artist should have at his command all manner of different means of expression, that he may be able to use his single tones, according to the expression required, with widely diverse qualities of resonance. This, too, must be cared for in his studies. But these studies, because they must fit each individual case, according to the genius or talent of the individual, can be imparted and directed only by a good teacher.

The head voice, when its value is properly appreciated, is the most valuable possession of all singers, male and female. It should not be treated as a Cinderella, or as a last resort,—as is often done too late, and so without results, because too much time is needed to regain it, when once lost,—but should be cherished and cultivated as a guardian angel and guide, like no other. Without its aid all voices lack brilliancy and carrying power; they are like a head without a brain. Only by constantly summoning it to the aid of all other registers is the singer able to keep his voice fresh and youthful. Only by a careful application of it do we gain that power of endurance which enables us to meet the most fatiguing demands. By it alone can we effect a complete equalization of the whole compass of all voices, and extend that compass.

This is the great secret of those singers who keep their voices young till they reach an advanced age. Without it all voices of which great exertions are demanded infallibly meet disaster. Therefore, the motto must be always, practice, and again, practice, to keep one's power uninjured; practice brings freshness to the voice, strengthens the muscles, and is, for the singer, far more interesting than any musical composition.

If in my explanations I frequently repeat myself, it is done not unintentionally, but deliberately, because of the difficulty of the subject, as well as of the superficiality and negligence of so many singers who, after once hastily glancing through such a treatise—if they consider it worth their while at all to inform themselves on the subject—think they have done enough with it.

One must read continually, study constantly by one's self, to gain even

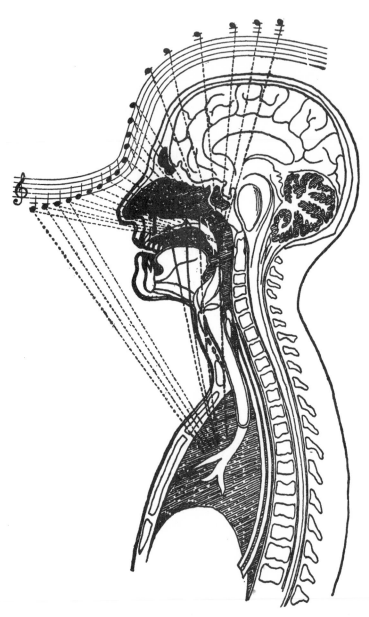

Dotted lines denote vocal sensations of soprano and tenor singers.

a faint idea of the difficulty of the art of singing, of managing the voice, and even of one's own organs and mistakes, which are one's second self. The phenomenon of the voice is an elaborate complication of manifold functions which are united in an extremely limited space, to produce a single tone; functions which can only be heard, scarcely felt—indeed, should be felt as little as possible. Thus, in spite of ourselves, we can only come back again to the point from which we started, as in an eddy, repeating the explanations of the single functions, and relating them to each other.

Since in singing we sense none of the various activities of the cartilage, muscles, ligaments, and tendons that belong to the vocal apparatus, feel them only in their coöperation, and can judge of the correctness of their workings only through the ear, it would be absurd to think of them while singing. We are compelled, in spite of scientific knowledge, to direct our attention while practising to the sensations of the voice, which are the only ones we can become aware of—sensations which are confined to the very palpable functions of the organs of breathing, the position of the nose, of the larynx, of the palate, of the diaphragmatic attacks and finally, to the sensation of the resonance of the head cavities. The perfect tone results from the combined operations of all these functions, the sensations of which I undertake to explain, and the control of which the ear alone can undertake.

This is the reason why it is so important to learn to hear one's self, and to sing in such a way that one can do so at all times.

Even in the greatest stress of emotion, the power of self-control must never be lost; you must never allow yourself to sing in a slovenly, that is, in a heedless way, or to exceed your powers, or even to reach their extreme limit. That would be synonymous with roughness, which should be excluded from every art, especially in the art of song. The listener must gain a pleasing impression from every tone, every expression of the singer, and the feeling that much more may be given if desired.

Strength must not be confounded with roughness; and the two must not go hand in hand together. Phenomenal beings may perhaps be permitted to go beyond the strength of others; but to the others this must remain forbidden. It cannot become a regular practice, and is best limited to the single phenomenon. We should otherwise soon reach the point of crudest realism, from which at best we are not far removed. Roughness will never attain artistic justification, not even in the case of the greatest individual singers, because it is an offence.

The public should witness from interpretative art only what is good and noble on which to form its taste; there should be nothing crude or commonplace put before it, which it might consider itself justified in taking as an example.

The low position of the larynx can easily be secured by pronouncing the vowel $\overline{oo}$; the high, by pronouncing the vowels $\bar{a}$ and $\bar{e}$. Often merely thinking of one or the other is enough to put the larnyx, tongue, and palate in the right relation to each other. Whenever I sing in a high vocal range, I can plainly feel the larynx rise and take a diagonal position by means of the tongue, which, however, only signifies a closer union of the organs, one with the other, and a higher position of the back of the tongue, as well as lowering or softening of the entire larynx. Nevertheless the energy of the tension increases from head to foot.

The movement is of course very slight. Yet I have the feeling in my throat as if everything in it were stretching lengthwise.

Sensation and Position of the Tongue

WE feel the placing of its tip against or beneath the front teeth; I place the tip very low, so that it really curves over in front. (See plate.)

Its hinder part must be drawn back toward the palate, in the pronunciation of every letter.

Furthermore, by looking in the mirror we can *see* that the sides of the tongue are raised as soon as we wish to form a soft furrow in it, that is, as we *must* do to produce the palatal resonance. (Only in the head tone without the added palatal or chest resonance has the tongue no furrow; it must, however, lie very high, since otherwise its mass, when it lies flat, presses against the larynx and produces pinches or otherwise disagreeable tones.) In the case of pupils where the tongue does not interfere with the tone, it is not absolutely necessary to create a furrow. There are pupils who by nature bring with them an exaggerated furrow which squeezes the upper part of the larynx. It must in that case be entirely removed.

The correct position of the tongue, preparatory to singing, is gained by saying the vowel sounds *äho*, $\overline{oo}$ as if about to yawn; but I consider it better to begin one's work with *āyē* and then with $\overline{oo}$ or to carefully connect all of them.

Correct   Incorrect

The tongue must not turn over upward with its tip. As soon as the tip has been employed in the pronunciation of the consonants *l, n, s, t,* and

47

z, in which its service is very short and sharp, it must return to its former position, and keep to it.

It is best to watch the movements of the tongue in the mirror until we have formed the correct habit permanently. The more elastic the tongue is in preparing the form for the breath to pass through, the stiller will it appear, the stiller will it feel to us. It is well, however, for a considerable time to watch in a mirror all functions of the organs that can be seen: the expression of the face, the position of the tongue, the position of the mouth, and the movement of the lips.

The Sensation of the Nose—the Nose Form

ONE of the most important positions closely connected with the first breath-jerk (see "How Do I Breathe," page 122) is produced by the dilation of the nostrils, the lifting and pushing of the backward nasal wall toward the so-broadened nose which in turn widens the pillars of the fauces and enables them to coöperate. The soft palate and the pillars of the fauces have a firm hold at the nose and a point of resistance upon which they can continually, according to necessity, heighten and lower themselves without having to change the position given them by this support.

As soon as the nose is adjusted by the breath-jerk and with it the $\bar{a}$ is placed by the larynx, the $y\bar{e}$ position must be joined to the $\bar{a}$; this brings the tone forward toward the nose and lets it ring over the lowered palate, as by means of the $y\bar{e}$ the tongue compels the larynx to take a higher backward position and thus constricts the cavity of the mouth. The sensation would appear thus: —a— horizontally alone and $\bar{a}y\bar{e}$ joined to it. The y and the $\bar{e}$ are felt firmly at the nasal wall. The slanting —a— which represents the frontal lowering of the larynx, pushes with its $\bar{a}$-strength toward the chest muscles in front and so, always replaced and rearticulated, comes to be placed under the strongly tensed nasal wall where it must always remain. All of this produces a particular position of the palate in relation to the nasal wall, which can be held even when the chin is lowered during pronunciation, or when making a short pause between tones and letters, in short, whenever it is necessary to loosen or relax. It sustains the connection of the entire muscular apparatus of mouth, throat, chest, and diaphragm, taking for granted that the renewed adjustment of the larynx is never forgotten.

To this continually held or renewed position of nose and palate, it is necessary to join and shut off all that concerns tone and word. This form must also continue to exist up to the completion of the tone. The hearer has distinct sensation of this, because the unceasing vibration of the breath

49

(produced by the strongly articulated $\bar{e}$) vibrating even after the completion of the tone, continues to suggest the vital sound both to singer and listener. The connecting muscles of this form, which must fit very firmly and elastically one to the other, must never for a moment neglect to give the tone-vitality and tone-coloring. This they do by making the larynx articulate unceasingly. New life is given to the tone chiefly by contracting and gently widening the never idle muscles of articulation as well as by the skilful increase and decrease of breath, which is naturally very closely connected with the process of articulation.

There is something very stable and very nasal in this connective form which can be widened without producing open tones, and which can be minimally closed without extinguishing tone and word.

On this the most wonderful of all tone-forms, which the nose chiefly creates and teaches us to sense, and in the coöperation of all contiguous muscles lies that which binds tone and word as I understand it and as I unceasingly do in my art of song.

By distending the nostrils the pillars of the fauces inflate. The nose therefore effects this function. Without the action of the nose it would remain inactive. The energetic drawing up of the tendons at the nose toward the eyes and forehead, and toward the temples and beyond to the ears while singing is an exceptionally important help. The vowels $\bar{e}$ and $\bar{a}$ especially demand this tensed nose position; but the singer does very well when he uses it with all other vowels and tones in order to preserve their ringing and carrying quality. We singers must therefore renew continually these given nose functions.

It happens that in the pronunciation of consonants (which must be pronounced in the $\bar{a}$ position) one must begin with $\bar{a}$ and end with it, as, for example, n—which must be pronounced in singing $\bar{a}n\bar{a}$—thus renewing the nose functions three times in one letter, not to speak of the very delicate wavelike nuances which have to be produced in the n-sound itself. All this is to make the letter resonant—more on this subject later. Nose and tongue function should be practised first. One should never forget that the nose allows the breath to escape only when the mouth is closed. As soon as the mouth is opened in singing the nose shuts off the exit of the breath through the nose so as to lead the breath back of the tongue to the head cavities. You can easily prove this by singing the vowel $\bar{e}$ and at the same time holding the nose shut with the fingers.

The Sensations of the Palate

THE sensations of the palate are best made clear to us by raising the softest part behind the nose. This part is situated very far back. Try touching it carefully with the finger. It is of immeasurable importance to the singer. By raising it the entire resonance of the head cavities is brought into play—consequently the head tones are produced. When it is raised, the surface of the pillars of the fauces is reduced in size. In its normal position it allows the pillars to be distended and to close off the head cavities from the throat, in order to produce the chest tones, that is, to permit the breath to make fullest use of the palatal and chest resonance. As soon as the soft palate is lowered under the nose, it makes a point of resonance for the middle range of voice, by permitting the overtones to resound at the same time in the nose.

The tongue and the palate perform the whole work as far as concerns the different resonances which can be united and separated by them, but must always work together in close relation, always bound together in all tones in all kinds of voices.

The lowest chest tones of the bass, the highest head tones of the soprano, are thus the two poles between which the entire gamut of all voices can be formed. From this it can be perceived that with a certain degree of skill and willingness to work, every voice will be capable of great extension.

The Sensation of the Resonance
of the Head Cavities

THE sensation of the resonance of the head cavities is perceived chiefly by those who are unaccustomed to using the head tones. The resonance against the occipital walls of the head cavities, when the head tones are employed, at first causes a very marked irritation of the nerves of the head and ear. But this disappears as soon as the singer gets accustomed to it. The head tones can be used and directed by the breath only with a clear head. The least depression such as comes with headaches, megrim, or moodiness may have the worst effect, or even make their use quite impossible. This feeling of oppression and dizziness is lost after regular conscious practice, by which all unnecessary and disturbing pressure is avoided.

In singing very high head tones, I have a feeling as if they lay high above the head, as if I were letting them off in the air, but, even so, they also have a connection with the larynx and the diaphragm. (See plate, page 9.)

Here, too, is the explanation of singing *in the neck*. The breath, in all high tones when much mixed with head tones or when using head tones only, passes very far back, directly from the throat into the cavities of the head, and thereby, and through the oblique position of the larynx, gives rise to the sensations just described. A singer who inhales and exhales carefully, that is, with knowledge of the physiological processes, will always have a certain feeling of pleasure, an attenuation in the throat as if it were stretching itself upward and downward. The bulging out of veins in the neck, that can so often be seen in singers, is as wrong as the swelling up of the neck, looks very ugly, and is not without danger from congestion.

With rapid scales one has the feeling of great firmness of the throat muscles; with trills, of a certain stiffness of the larynx. (See "Trill," pp. 103ff.) An unsteady movement of the latter, this way and that, would be disadvantageous to the trill, to rapid scales, as well as to the cantilena. For this reason, because the changing movements of the organs must go on quite imperceptibly and inaudibly, it must be more like a shifting than a movement. In rapid scales the lowest tone must be "placed" with a view to the production of the highest, and in descending, the greatest care must be exercised that the tones shall produce the sensation of closely connected sounds, through being bound to the high tone position and pressed toward the nose with the sensation of pushing them higher and narrower.

In this all the participating vocal organs must be able to keep up a muscular contraction, often very rigid, the form remaining tensed, one organ to another. And in this tension one or the other vocal organ, as larynx, tongue, diaphragm, palate, or nose, must act with especial elasticity or especial strength, according to the necessity of accent or according to the physical condition of the singer. Only gradually through long years of careful and regular study is it to be achieved. Excessive practice is of no use in this—only regular and intelligent practice—and success comes only in course of time.

Never should the muscular contractions become convulsive and produce pressure which the muscles cannot endure for a long time. They must respond to all necessary demands upon their strength, yet remain elastic in order that, easily relaxing or again contracting, they may promptly adapt themselves to every nuance in tone and accent desired by the singer.

A singer can become and continue to be master of his voice and means of expression only as long as he practises daily conscious vocal gymnastics. In this way alone can he obtain unconditional mastery over his muscles, and, through them, of the finest controlling apparatus, of the beauty of his voice, as well as of the art of song as a whole.

Training the muscles of the vocal organs so that their power to contract and relax to all desired degrees of strength, throughout the entire gamut of the voice, is always at command makes the master singer.

On Vocal Position—There Are No Vocal Registers—Propagation-Form

WHAT is a vocal register? Only a vocal position. A series of tones sung in a certain way, which are produced by a certain position of the vocal organs—larynx, tongue, and palate. Every voice includes three positions—chest, middle, and head. But all are not employed in every class of voice.

Two of them are often found connected to a certain extent in beginners; the third is usually much weaker, or does not exist at all. Only very rarely is a voice found naturally equalized over its whole compass.

Do registers exist by nature? No. It may be said that they are created through long years of speaking in the vocal range that is easiest to the person, or in one adopted by imitation, which then becomes a fixed habit. If this is coupled with a natural and proper working of the muscles of the vocal organs, it may become the accustomed range, strong in comparison with others, and form a register by itself. This fact would naturally be appreciated only by singers.

If, on the other hand, the muscles are wrongly employed in speaking, not only the range of voice generally used, but the whole voice as well, may be made to sound badly. So, in every voice, one or another range may be stronger or weaker; and this is, in fact, almost always the case, since mankind speaks and sings in the pitch easiest or most accustomed, without giving thought to the proper position of the organs in relation to each other; and people are rarely made to pay attention as children to speaking clearly and in an agreeable voice. In the most fortunate instances the range thus practised reaches limits on both sides, not so much those of the person's power, as those set by his lack of skill, or practice. Limitations are put on the voice through taking account only of the easiest and most accustomed thing, without inquiring into the potentialities of the organs or the demands of art.

(Bass and baritone.)

Covered tones for bass and
baritone.

(Soprano, contralto, and tenor.)

Covered tones for contralto and
soprano.

Change of attack.
(Bass and baritone.)

Change of attack.
(Soprano, contralto, and tenor.)

Now, suppose such a peculiarity, which includes, let us say, three or four tones, is extended to six or eight, then, in the course of time, in the worst cases, a break is produced at the outside limits. In the most favorable cases the tones lying next beyond these limits are conspicuously weak and without power compared with those previously forced.

Three such limits or ways of singing can be found and used. Chest, middle, and head voice—all three form registers when exaggerated, but they should be shaded off and melt into each other. The organs, through the skilful training of the teacher, as well as by the exercise of the pupil's talent and industry, must be accustomed to taking such positions that one vocal position leads into another imperceptibly. In this way beauty, equality, and increased compass of the voice will be made to enhance its usefulness.

This striking contrast of the different vocal ranges has given them the name of "register." These are everywhere accepted as a matter of course, and for years have been a terror in the teaching of singing, that has done more than anything else to create a dreadful bewilderment among singers and teachers. To eradicate it is probably hopeless. Yet, these registers are nothing more than three disconnected manners of using the vocal and resonating apparatus.

With all the bad habits of singers, with all the complete ignorance of cause and effect that prevail, it is not surprising that some pretend to tell us that there are two, three, four, or five registers. It will be much more correct to call every tone of every voice by the name of a new additional register, for in the end, every tone will and *must* be taken in a different relation, with a different position of the organs, although the difference may be imperceptible, if it is to have its proper place in the whole. People cling to the appellations of chest, middle, and head *register*, confounding vocal position with register, and making a hopeless confusion, from which only united and very powerful forces can succeed in extricating them.

As long as the word "register" is kept in use, the registers will not disappear. And yet, the register question must be swept away, to give place to another class of ideas, sounder views on the part of teachers, and a truer conception on the part of singers and pupils.

Naturally a singer can devote more strength to the development of one or two connected ranges of his voice than to a voice perfectly equalized in all its accessible ranges. For this are required many years of the most patient study and observation, often a long-continued or entire sacrifice of one or the other limit of a range for the benefit of the adjacent weaker one; of the head voice especially, which, if unmixed, sounds uneven and thin in comparison with the middle range until, by means of practised elasticity of the organs, endurance of the throat muscles, muscular tension of the organs in relative position, a positive equalization can take place.

Voices which contain only one or two positions are called short voices, for their availability is as limited as they are themselves.

Yet it must be remembered that all voices alike, whether short or long, even those of the most skilful singers, when age comes on, are apt to lose their highest ranges, if they are not continually practised throughout their entire compass with the subtlest use of the head tones. Thence it is to be concluded that a singer ought always to extend the compass of his voice as far as possible, in order to be certain of possessing the compass that he needs.

On the formation of the organs depends much of the character of the voice. There are strong, weak, deep, and high voices by nature; but every voice, by means of proper study, can attain a certain degree of strength, flexibility, and compass.

Unfortunately, stubbornness enters largely into this question, and often works in opposition to the teacher. Many, for instance, wish to be altos, either because they are afraid of ruining their voices by working for a higher compass, or because it is easier for them, even if their voices are not altos at all.

Nowadays operas are no longer composed for particular singers and the special characteristics of their voices. Composers and librettists express what they feel without regard to an alto singer who has no high c or a soprano who has no low a flat or g. But the artist will always find what he needs.

Different ranges exist in the voices of almost all singers, but they ought not to be heard, ought not, indeed, to exist. Everything should be sung with a mixed voice in such a way that no tone is forced at the expense of any other. To avoid monotony the singer should have at his disposal a wealth of means of expression in all ranges of his voice. (See the chapters on vowels.) Before all else he should have knowledge of the advantages in the resonance of certain tones, and of their connection with each other. The *soul* must be expressed by vowel coloring, muscular tension, and relaxation; skill and knowledge as to cause and effect, management of the breath, and perfection of the throat formation must give the power to produce every dynamic gradation and detail of expression. Registers are, accordingly, produced when the singer forces a series of tones, generally ascending, upon one and the same resonating point, instead of remembering that in a progression of tones no one tone can be exactly like another, because the position of the organs must be different for each. The palate must remain elastic from the front teeth to its hindmost part, mobile and

susceptible, though imperceptibly, to all changes. Very much depends on
the continuous harmony of action of the soft palate and nose, which
must always be in full evidence, the raising and extension of the former
producing changes in the tone. If, as often happens when the registers are
sharply defined, tones fall into a *cul de sac,* escape into another register is
impossible, without a jump, which may lead to disaster. With every tone
that the singer has to sing, he must always have the feeling that he *can* go
higher and that the attack for different tones must not be forced upon one
and the same point.

The larynx must not be *suddenly* pressed down nor jerked up, except
when this is desired as a special effect. That is, when one wishes to make
a transition—*legato,* from a chest tone to a tone in the middle or head
register, as the old Italians used to do, and as I, too, learned to do,
thus:—

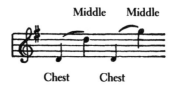

It is solely the counter-attack of the diaphragm toward the larynx—*ā*
which depends on the upward stroke, on the breath pressure, which allows
the larynx to spring up suddenly. This was called breaking the tone; it was
very much used, and gave fine effects when it was well done. I use it to-
day, especially in Italian music, where it belongs. It is an exception to the
rule for imperceptible or inaudible change of position of the organs—that
it should not be made *suddenly.*

The scale proceeds from one semitone to another; each is different;
each, as you go on, requires greater height, wherefore the position of the
organs cannot remain the same for several different tones. But, as there
should never be an abrupt change audible in the way of singing, so should
there never be an abrupt change felt in the sensation of the singer's throat.
Every tone must be imperceptibly prepared in an elastic channel that is
relaxed, placed, and again relaxed, and must produce an easy feeling in
the singer, as well as an agreeable impression upon the listener.

The small peak indicated in the illustration is enormously extensible
and can be shifted into infinite varieties of position. However unimportant
its raising and lowering may appear, they are nevertheless of great
importance for the tone and the singer. The focal point of the breath, that
forms simultaneously the attack and the body of the tone, by the operation

of the abdominal breath pressure against the chest, is always firmly placed on, beneath, or behind the nose. Without body even the finest *pianissimo* has no significance. The very highest unmixed head tones are an exception, and they can express nothing. There can be no body expected in them. Their soaring quality of sound endures no pressure, and consequently gives no expression, which is possible only through an admixture of palatal and chest resonance by means of dark vowels. Their only significance is gained through their pure euphony.

All vowels, too, must keep their point of resonance uninterruptedly on the palate. All beauty in the art of song in the cantilena as well as in all technique, rests chiefly in uninterrupted connection between the tone and the word, in the flexible connection of the soft palate with the hard, in the continually elastic adjustment of the former to the latter.

If the singer wishes to control his tone—and in practising he must always do so—he needs only to test it to see whether he can easily make it softer without perceptible change in the position of the organs, and carry it higher toward the nose and the cavities of the forehead, that is, prepare a form for its continuation upward.

In this way he can learn how much height a tone needs without being too high, and how much it often lacks in height and duration to sound high enough.

In this way remarkable faults become evident! The reason why a tone sounds too low is that the pillars of the fauces are raised too high toward the back, or that the back of the tongue lies too low, which together create a hole in the cavity of the mouth, preventing the head voice from vibrating with the tone. This fault is met with in very many singers, in all kinds of voices, and in almost the same places. It comes only from an unyielding retention of the same resonating point for several tones, and a failure to bring in the resonance of the head cavities. The "propagation form," or continuing form,[1] must always be prepared consciously, for without it artistic singing is not to be thought of.

The neglect of this most important principle usually results in overstraining the vocal cords and throat muscles. This is followed first by singing flat, and later by the appearance of the hideous tremolo (see "The Tremolo," pp. 70ff.) to which so many singers fall victims.

---

[1] "Fortpflanzungsform": the preparation made in the vocal organs for taking the next tone before leaving the one under production, so that the succeeding tones shall all be of like character and quality.

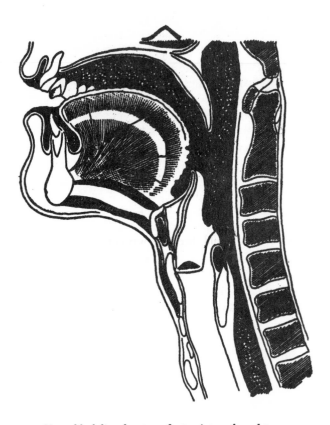

Heavy black line denotes softest point on the palate.

White Voices

THERE are also singers, male and female, who use too much head tone through their entire compass. Such voices are called white. Their use of the dark palatal resonance and of the chest and diaphragm tensions and attacks being insufficient, they are not able to make a deeper impression, because their power of expression is practically nothing. In such cases it would be advisable to raise the pillars of the fauces a little higher, and place the larynx somewhat lower, and to mingle judiciously with all the other vowels, the vowel sound $\overline{oo}$, that requires a lower position of the larynx. The voices would become warmer and would sound more expressive. As soon as the singer is able to create easily, inaudibly, and consciously on every tone that correct propagation form for the next tone, all questions as to register must disappear. He must not, however, be drilled on *registers*; several tones must not be forced on one and the same point. Every tone should be put naturally into its own place; should receive the pitch, duration, and strength it needs for its perfection. And one master rules it all—the ear!

The goal is, unfortunately, seldom reached because it can be reached only through the moderation that comes from mastery; and, alas! only true masters practise it.

It may be accepted as true that the lower ranges of the voice have the greatest strength, the middle ranges the greatest power of expression, the higher the greatest carrying power.

The best mixture—all three together—may be developed to the highest art by the skill of the individual, often, indeed, only by a good ear for it. Whenever expression of the word's significance, beauty of the vocal material, and perfection of phrasing are found united in the highest degree, it is due either to knowledge or to a natural skill in the innumerable ways of fitting the sung word to the particular resonance—connections that are suitable to realize its significance, and hence its spirit. They are brought out by a stronger inclination toward one or the other of the resonance surfaces by means of mixed vowels without, however, injuring the connection or the beauty of the musical phrase. Here æsthetic feeling plays the chief part, for whatever may be its power and its truthfulness, the result must always be beautiful, that is, restrained within proper limits.

This law, too, remains the same for all voices. It is a question of the entire compass of a voice trained for artistic singing, one that is intrusted with the greatest of tasks, to interpret works of art that are not popular songs, but, for the most part, human tragedies. Most male singers—tenors especially—consider it beneath them, generally, indeed, unnatural or ridiculous, to use the falsetto, which is a part of all male voices, as the head tones are a part of all female voices. They do not understand how to make use of its assistance, because they often have no idea of its existence, or know it only in its unmixed purity, that is, its thinnest quality. Of its proper application, that is, its necessary admixture with chest resonance, they have not the remotest conception. Their singing is generally in keeping with their ignorance.

The mixture is present by nature in all kinds of voices, but singers must possess the skill and knowledge to employ it, else the natural advantage goes for nothing.

Theodor Wachtel and the Vocal
Technique of Tenors

THE most perfect singer that I remember in my Berlin experience was
Theodor Wachtel, in this respect, that with his voice of rare splendor he
united all that vocal art which, as it seems, is destined quite to disappear
from among us. How beautiful were his coloratura, his trills—simply
flawless! Phrasing, force, fulness of tone, and beauty were perfect,
musically without a blemish. If he did not go outside the range of Arnold,
George Brown, Stradella, Vasco, the Postilion, and Lionel, it was probably
because he felt that he was not equal to interpreting the Wagnerian spirit.
In this he was very wise. As one of the first of vocal artists, whose voice
was superbly trained and was preserved to the end of his life, I have had
to pay to Wachtel the tribute of the most complete admiration and
recognition, in contrast to many others who thought themselves greater
than he, and yet were not worthy to unloose the latchet of his shoes.

Recently the little Italian tenor Bonci has won my hearty admiration
for his splendidly equalized voice, his perfect art, and his knowledge of
his resources; and notwithstanding the almost ludicrous figure that he cut
in serious parts, he elicited hearty applause. Cannot German tenors, too,
learn to sing *well*, even if they do interpret Wagner? Will they not learn,
for the sake of this very master, that it is their duty not to use their voices
recklessly?

Is it not disrespectful toward our greatest masters that they always have
to play hide and seek with the *bel canto*, the trill, and coloratura? Not till
one has fully realized the difficulties of the art of song does it really
become of value and significance. Not till then are one's eyes opened to
the duty owed not only to one's self but to the public.

The appreciation of a difficulty makes study doubly attractive; the
laborious ascent of a summit which no one can contest, is the attainment
of a goal.

Voices in which the palatal resonance—and so, power—is the predominating factor are the hardest to manage and to preserve. They are generally called chest voices. Uncommon power and fulness of tone in the middle ranges are extremely seductive. Only rarely are people found with sense enough to renounce such an excess of fulness in favor of the head tones, that is the least risky range to exploit and preserve, even if this has to be done only temporarily.

Copious vocal resources may be brought before the public with impunity and thereby submitted to strain only after long and regular study.

The pure head tone, without admixture of palatal resonance, is feeble, close at hand, but penetrating and of carrying power equalled by no other. Palatal resonance without admixture of the resonance of the head cavities (head tones) makes the tone very powerful when heard near by, but without vibrancy for a large auditorium. This is the best proof of how greatly every tone needs the proper admixture.

The Highest Head Tones—Staccato

As we have already seen, there is almost no limit to the height that can be reached by the pure head tone without admixture of palatal resonance. Very young voices, especially, can reach such heights, for without any strain they possess the necessary adaptability and skill in the adjustment to each other of the larynx, tongue, and pillars of the fauces. A skill that rests on ignorance of the true nature of the phenomenon must be called pure chance, and thus its disappearance is as puzzling to teacher and listener as its appearance had been in the first place. How often is it paired with a total lack of ability to produce anything but the highest head tones! As a general rule such voices have a very short lease of life, because their possessors are exploited as wonders, before they have any conception of the way to use them, of tone, right singing, and of cause and effect in general. An erroneous pressure of the muscles, a wrong movement of the tongue, an attempt to increase the strength of the tone, all these things extinguish quickly and for all time the wonder-singer's little light.

We Lehmann children in our youth could sing to the very highest pitch. It was nothing for my sister Marie to strike the 4-line *g* a hundred times in succession, and trill on it for a long time. She could have sung in public at the age of seven. But since our voices, through the circumstances of our life and surroundings, were forced to early exertions, they lost their remarkable high notes; yet enough was left to sing the *Queen of Night* (in Mozart's opera "Die Zauberflöte"), with the high *f*.

But one should not suppose that the pure head tones have no power. When they are properly used, their vibrancy is a substitute for any amount of power, and mixed with chest resonance they can create very strong tones.

As soon as the head tones come into consideration, one should *never* attempt to sing an open *ah*, because on *ah* the tongue lies flattest. One should think of an *ā*, and in the highest range even an *ē*; should mix the

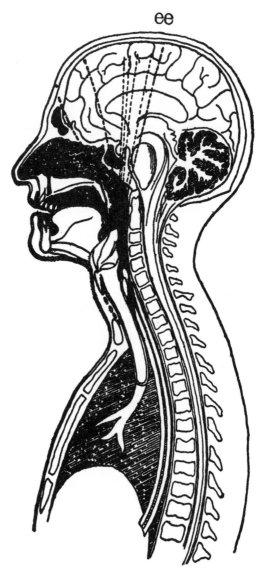

Dotted lines denote vocal sensation in the highest head tones
without mixture.

ā and *ē* with *ōō*, and thereby produce a position of the tongue and soft palate that makes the path clear for the introduction of the breath into the cavities of the head.

Singers who, on the other hand, pronounce *ā* and *ē* too sharply, need only introduce an admixture of *ōō*; they thereby lower the position of the larynx, and thus give the vowel and tone a darker color.

Since the stream of breath in the highest tones produces currents whirling with great rapidity, the more rapidly the higher is the tone, the slightest pressure that may injure the form in which they circulate may ruin the evenness of the tone, its pitch, perhaps the tone itself. Each high tone must *soar gently*, like the overtones.

The upper limits of a bass and baritone voice are

where, consequently, the tones must be mixed. Pure head tones, that is, falsetto, are never demanded higher than this. I regard it, however, as absolutely necessary for the artist to give consideration to his falsetto, that he may include it among his known resources. Neither a bass nor a baritone should neglect to give it the proper attention, and both should learn to use it as one of their most important auxiliary forces.

With what mastery did Betz make use of it; how noble and beautiful his voice sounded in all its ranges; of what even strength it was, and how infallibly fresh! And let no one believe that Nature gave it to him thus. As a beginner in Berlin he was quite unsatisfactory. He had the alternative given him either to study with great industry or to seek another engagement, for his successor had already been selected. Betz chose to devote himself zealously to study; he began also to play the 'cello; he learned to *hear*, and finally raised himself to be one of our first singers, in many rôles never to be forgotten. Betz knew, like myself, many things that to-day are neither taught nor learned. (See section on Pronunciation.)

In Berlin, in the part of *Matilde* in "Wilhelm Tell," I frequently played a joke on the audience by holding, in a cadenza, the high *e* flat with mixed voice (voix mixte) then once more decreasing the already diminished breath, I slowly closed the mouth and so in a shut-off space let the uninterrupted tone resound. I remember how the audience in the parquet suddenly looked about, thinking it had heard an echo which my tone resembled precisely. In slow or fast runs up to high *d*, *e* flat, *e*, *f* a certain amount of tension can still be retained, which by articulating $\bar{a}$ unites the muscles of the nose, larynx, chest, and diaphragm, naturally with stationary breath pressure, that is, with a decreasing stream of breath. The slightest breath pressure would destroy the highest notes.

The greatest breath tension and the counter-tension of the diaphragm decrease with the exaggerated height of the highest head tone but the form endures. The tongue lies broad, comfortable. The higher you wish to go the more an $\bar{e}$ must be articulated under the tongue backward in the throat, but it must never be pressed. Under it you may even think a relaxed $\overline{oo}$. But in descending a scale or run, the loosely held $\bar{e}$ is gradually held in place by the energetic $\bar{a}$ and y support pushed higher up toward the nasal wall and considerably heightened, because the downward-going tones are apt to become too low in pitch, if the singer imagines them as descending. Each of the descending tones must be doubly heightened, whether it be by means of an $\bar{e}$-point, or relaxation, or by the constriction of tongue and palate. Then, too, the $\bar{a}$ must gradually be pronounced against the breath pressure; it serves as a support to the $\bar{e}$ as it is heightened and made narrower toward the back. To return to the highest head tones, which are best located by entirely closing the mouth, they are born of the very highest voix mixte. The connection of the nose and larynx with the diaphragm, that is, a vertically narrow line, may be but delicately sensed. The chest and breath pressure have become quite still and immobile. Here nothing must push or move forward. The larynx, too, should barely articulate an $\bar{a}$. All is placed on a most relaxed $\bar{e}$ in a long, united, and stationary form. There is only left remaining the thought of $\bar{o}$, $y\bar{e}$, and $\overline{oo}$ which take up the delicate work, resting on a stationary breath pressure, on a totally diminished breath. With all this delicate work the incessant articulation of $\bar{e}$ has to sustain the tone as well as the breath streaming in the back.

The larynx adjusts itself loosely and broadly under the tongue which has accommodated itself easily to the tone-height. Both close off, as it were, the pharynx from the cavity of the chest and the throat. There is no strong sensation of tension, which the palate also seems scarcely capable of putting in evidence. Nevertheless this tension must be made use of in every direction.

But a little of the upward, backward, streaming breath vibrates in the head. We hear wonderfully fine violin tones, and, made with a closed mouth—which I would rather call the echo-form—it brings to the ear, as ringing from a great distance, the music of the spheres.

Such tones may be held a long time and even given some body by opening the mouth slowly and distinctly articulating; and with the $\bar{a}$ and *ē* they may very skilfully be transformed into voix mixte. What could not be accomplished if one lived long enough!

With these uppermost head resonances I, to this day, sing the highest *a* and *b* flat, providing I have no catarrh. I can strike them many times in succession and with open mouth, without making use of the echo-form that I have often shown my pupils. All of my pupils, even the altos, sing the great scale, slowly up and down their entire range, going up to high *f* and *g*. One young soprano thereby produces, in singing staccato, magnificent, strong flageolet tones due to the peculiarity of her voice enabling her to carry her *äh* (otherwise very deficient) very loosely along the palate to the very highest position.

Staccato

The staccato can be produced in various ways, according to accidental and individual, or habitual and skilful form adjustment. Above all it is necessary to have the free, let us say, hollow ōō-form made by the nose, palate, and diaphragm. It may be thought very far front, and also, according to the individual, very far back. Nose and palate form a high, tightly tensed saddle upon which all the work, called forth by all the muscles of the organs, plays. This saddle is the opposite pole to the diaphragm and these together make the bell-shaped form. As soon as the form is adjusted, the clapper, that is the larynx, strongly tensed with *ā*, strikes into this hollow ōō-form together with the chest muscles, striking like a ball that hits the mark in the target.

The diaphragm, which must not in this case act antagonistically to the larynx attack, holds firmly the lower end of the form. Just as in the case of the breath-jerk this form with the breath becomes rigid as long as the staccati are being made. The mouth remains open even during the pauses between the staccati strokes, as only silent pauses occur between the single wordless tones. No respiration takes place. For example: breath-jerk—pause—stroke—pause—stroke—pause, etc.

In any case the nostrils gently inflated on ōō must be connected, bell shaped, with the pillars of the fauces. The form continues to remain hollow until the clapper with the *ā* attack strikes into it, and, in doing so, particularly calls in the coöperation of the chest muscles every time it strikes. Those who, with this form adjustment of the fauces, can very gently close off the pharynx very far back with the tongue, will be able, without articulation, the thought only dwelling on ōō or *ē*, to produce very good flageolet tones and the very highest head tones.

The Tremolo

BIG voices produced by large, strong organs through which the breath can flow in a broad, powerful stream, are easily disposed to suffer from the tremolo, because the outflow of the breath against the vocal cords occurs too immediately. The breath is sent there directly from the diaphragm instead of being driven by abdominal pressure forward against the chest, the controlling apparatus, from whence it, in minimal quantity and under control, is admitted to the vocal cords. Even the strongest vocal cords cannot for any length of time stand the uncontrolled pressure of the breath, that is, the direct breath pressure. One must learn to tense them by means of the various muscular functions.

In inhaling, the chest should be raised not at all or but very little— unless an exercise for the expansion of the chest is to be made of it. The pressure of the breath against the chest must be maintained as long as it is desired to sustain a tone or sing a phrase. As soon as the elastic abdominal and chest pressure ceases, the tone and the breath are at an end. Not till toward the very end of the breath, that is, of the tone or the phrase, should the pressure be slowly relaxed and the chest slowly sink, although tone- and word-form must continue to remain even beyond the end.

While I am singing, I must press the breath against the chest evenly, for in this way alone can it be directed evenly against the vocal cords, which action is the chief factor in a steady tone and in the only possible and proper use of the vocal cords. Control of the breath should never cease. Only in the beginning of singing does the chest—against which the breath is pushed—start to slowly inflate, reaching its greatest distention only when the breath phrase is ended. Then the chest slowly sinks. The tone should never be made stronger or weaker beyond the control of it, but the breath must always be decreased. This should be an inflexible rule for the singer.

I direct my whole attention to the pressure against the chest, which forms the door of the supply chamber of breath. Thence I admit to the vocal cords uninterruptedly only just so much as I wish to admit. I must not be stingy, nor yet extravagant with it. Besides giving steadiness, the pressure against the chest (the controlling apparatus) establishes the strength and the duration of the tone.

Upon the proper control and the continual articulation depends the

Vocal Cords

length of the breath, which, without interruption, rises from here, vibrates in the resonating chambers, and, kept in check in the elastic form of the resonating apparatus, obeys our will through articulation.

It can now be seen how easily the vocal cords can be injured by an uncontrolled current of breath, if it is directed against them in all its force. One need only see a picture of the vocal cords to understand the folly of exposing these delicate little bands to the explosive force of the breath. They cannot be protected too much; and also they cannot be too carefully exercised. They must be spared all work not properly theirs. This must be left to the resistance and tension of the chest muscles which in time learn to endure an out-and-out thump.

The tremolo can also be produced by the false placement of the larynx which is not always fixed close enough under the nose and chin, and being disunited with $\bar{e}$ and $\overline{oo}$ by means of y it wabbles about alone. The only remedy here is the energetic placement of the larynx with $\bar{a}$, that is, the placement of the tension of the chest and diaphragm muscles, which must always be renewed by continually articulating the $\bar{a}$. It might possibly come from the inactivity of the diaphragmatic muscles which do not make a counter-movement, that is, do not coöperate with the upper organs. This fact must be investigated by the teacher.

Even the vibrato, to which full voices are prone, should be nipped in the bud, for gradually the tremolo, and later something even worse, is developed from it. Life can be infused into the tone by means of vowel-mixing, a way that will do no harm.

Vibrato is the first stage, tremolo the second and much more hopeless, which shows itself in flat singing on the upper middle tones of the register. Referable in the same way to the over-burdening of the vocal cords is the excessive straining of the throat muscles, which through continual constriction lose their power of elastic contraction and relaxation, because pitch and duration of the tone are gained in an incorrect way, by forcing. Neither should be forced; pitch should be merely maintained soaring, as it were; strength should not be gained by cramped compression of the throat muscles, but by the completest possible filling with breath of the breath-form and the resonance chambers, under the government of the controlling apparatus, and that means a decrease of breath.

The more violent the exertions are made to force pitch and duration, the worse are the results. For most of the unhappy singers who do this, there is but one result: the voice is lost.

If the first and second stages of tremolo are difficult to remedy because the causes are rarely understood and the proper measures to take still more rarely, the repair of the last stage of the damage is nothing less than a fight in which only an unspeakable patience can win the victory.

The Cure

THERE are no magic cures for the singer. Only slowly, vibration upon vibration, can the true pitch be won back. In the word "soaring" lies the whole idea of the work. No more may the breath be allowed to flow uncontrolled through the wearied vocal cords; it must be forced against the chest, always, as if it were to come directly out thence. The throat muscles must lie fallow until they have lost the habit of cramped contraction, until the overtones again soar as they should, and are kept soaring long, though quite *piano*. At first this seems quite impossible, and is indeed very difficult, demanding all the patient's energy. But it is possible, and he cannot avoid it, for it is the only way to a thorough cure. The patient has an extremely disagreeable period to pass through. If he is industrious and careful, he will soon find it impossible to sing in his old way; but the new way is for the most part quite unfamiliar to him, because his ear still hears as it has previously been accustomed to hear. It may be that years will pass before he can again use the muscles, so long maltreated. But he should not be dismayed at this prospect. If he can no longer use his voice in public as a singer, he certainly can as a teacher— for *a teacher must be able to sing well.* How should he describe to others sensations in singing which he himself never felt? Is it not as if he undertook to teach a language that he did not speak himself? or an instrument that he did not play himself? When he himself does not hear, how shall he teach others to hear?

The degree of the evil, and the patient's skill, naturally have much to do with the rapidity of the cure. But one cannot throw off a habit of years' standing like an old garment; and every new garment, too, is uncomfortable at first. One cannot expect an immediate cure, either of himself or of others. If the singer undertakes it with courage and energy, he learns to use his voice with conscious understanding, as should have been done in the beginning.

And he must make up his mind to it, that even after a good cure, the old habits will reappear, whenever he is not in good form physically. That should not lead to discouragement; persistence will bring success.

As I have already said, singers with disabled voices like best to try "magic cures"; and there are teachers and pupils who boast of having effected such magic cures in a few weeks or hours.

Of them I give warning! and *equally*, of unprincipled physicians who daub around in the larynx, burn it, cut it, and make everything worse instead of better.

There is no other remedy than a slow, very careful study of the *causes* of the trouble, which in almost all cases consists in lack of control of the stream of breath through the vocal cords, and in disregard of the head tones, that is, of the over-tones; as well as in forcing the pitch and power of the tone upon a wrong resonating point of the palate, and in constricting the throat muscles. In these points all mistakes are almost invariably to be looked for; and in the recognition of them the proper means for correcting them are already indicated.

The cure is difficult and tedious. It needs an endless patience on the part of the sufferer as well as of the physician—that is, of the pupil and the *singing teacher* (the only proper physician for this disease)—because the nerves of the head are already sufficiently unstrung through the consciousness of their incapacity; yet they should be able to act easily and without effort in producing the head tones.

The repairing of a voice requires the greatest sympathetic appreciation and circumspection on the part of the teacher, who should always inspire the pupil with courage; and on the part of the pupil, all his tranquillity, nervous strength, and patience, in order to reach the desired goal.

Where there is a will there is a way!

The Tongue

SINCE it is the function of the tongue to conduct the column of breath above the larynx to the resonance chambers, too much attention cannot be given to it and its position, in speaking as well as in singing. If it lies too high or too low, it may, by constricting the breath, produce serious changes in the tone, making it pinched or even shutting it off entirely as soon as it presses on the larynx.

It has an extremely delicate and difficult task to perform. It must be in such a position as not to press either upon the larynx or epiglottis. Tongue and larynx must keep out of each other's way, although they always work in coöperation; but one must not hamper the other, and when one can withdraw no farther out of the way, the other must take it upon itself to do so. For this reason the back of the tongue must be raised high, the larynx stand low.

The tongue must generally form a furrow. With the lowest tones it lies relatively flattest, the tip *always* against and beneath the front teeth, so that the back of the tongue may freely rise and sink. Strong and yet delicate, it must be able to fit any letter of the alphabet; that is, help form its sound. It must be of the greatest sensitiveness in adapting itself to every tonal vibration, it must assist every change of tone and letter as quick as a flash and with unerring accuracy; without changing its position too soon or remaining too long in it, in the highest range it must be able almost to speak consonants out in the air.

With all its strength and firmness the tongue must be of the utmost sensitiveness toward the breath, which, as I have often said, must not be subjected to the least pressure above the larynx or in the larynx itself. Pressure must be limited to the abdominal and chest muscles; and this should better be called stress than pressure.

Without hindrance the column of breath, at its upper end like diverging rays of light, must fill and expand all the mucous membranes with its vibrations equally, diffuse itself through the resonance chambers, and penetrate the cavities of the head.

When the back of the tongue can rise no higher, the larynx must be lowered. This often happens in the highest ranges, and one needs only to mingle an $\overline{oo}$ in the vowel to be sung, which must not, however, be felt with deep-set larynx forward in the mouth but *behind the nose*. When the larynx must stand very low, the tongue naturally must not be *too* high, else it would affect the position of the larynx. One must learn to feel and hear it. To keep the larynx, the back of the tongue, and the palate always in readiness to offer mutual assistance, must become a habit.

I, for instance, after every syllable, at once jerk my tongue with tremendous power back to its normal position in singing; that is, with its

tip below the front teeth and the base raised. That goes on

constantly, as quick as a flash. At the same time my larynx takes such a position that the tongue cannot interfere with it, that is, press upon it.

The bad, bad tongue! one is too thick, another too thin, a third too long, a fourth much too short.

Ladies and gentlemen, these are nothing but the excuses of the lazy!

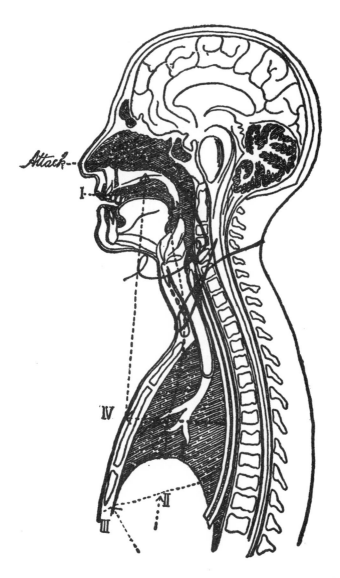

Heavy black and dotted lines denote that with the inspiration of breath: I, the diaphragm is sensibly stretched backward; II, enlarges the capacity of the chest by the drawing down of its floor; III, and so forms the supply chamber for the breath; IV, indicates the pressure of the breath against the chest tension muscle; V, the attack.

The Position of the Mouth
(Contraction of the Muscles of Speech)

WHAT must my sensations be with the muscles of speech? How shall I control them?

The best position of the mouth, the means of securing the proper use of the muscles of speech and of the vocal organs, is established by pronouncing the vowel $\bar{a}$, not too sharply, in the middle range of the voice, and trying to retain the position of the muscles after the sound has ceased.

This cannot be done without a *smiling* position of the mouth, consequently with a strong contraction of the muscles of the mouth, tongue, and throat, which can be felt to be drawn up as far as the ears.

In doing so the tongue—as far as the tip—lies at nearly an even height to the back, , the soft palate soars without arching, but rather somewhat depressed over it.

In pronouncing the vowels $\bar{a}$ and $\bar{e}$, the bright vowels, the up-flowing stream of the breath in the given position can only partly pass between the tongue and the palate. The other part is forced—unless the larynx stands too high—above the palate into the nasal cavities, to seek its opportunity for resonance.

The path for $\bar{a}$ and $\bar{e}$ above the palate is worthy of all attention as a place for the overtones of the middle voice. If the soft palate, in the lower middle tones, is forced too far toward the hard palate, the covered tones are without vibrancy. One must needs secure the help of the nose especially, when the palate is sunk beneath the nose, by inflating the nostrils and so entirely closing the nose.

I repeat the warning, not to force several tones upon the same resonating point, but to see that upon each tone the form necessary for succeeding tones is prepared. Neglect of this will sooner or later be paid for dearly.

Again, and always, attention must be given that in singing, and in speaking as well, nothing shall be cramped or held tense, except the pressure of the breath against the chest. It is of the utmost importance to maintain this position for *all* vowels, with the least possible perceptible modifications.

How can this be done? A and *e* are bright vowels, must be sung with a pleasant, almost smiling, position of the mouth. $\overline{Oo}$ and *o*, on the contrary, are dark vowels, for which the lips must be drawn into a sort of spout. Look at the position of the throat in these vowels: (1) as they are usually sung and spoken; (2) as I feel it, in singing, as I sing them, and as they must be sung and felt.

Connection of Vowels

How do I connect them with each other? If I wish to connect closely together two vowels that lie near to or far from each other, I must first establish the muscular contractions for $\bar{a}$, and introduce between the two vowels, whether they lie near together or far apart, a very well-defined y. Then (supposing, for instance, that I want to connect $\bar{a}$ and $\bar{e}$) I must join the $\bar{a}$ closely to the y, and the y closely to the e, so that there is not the least resonating space between the two that is not filled during the changes in the position of the organs, however carefully this is undertaken. There must be no empty space, no useless escape of breath, between any two of the sounds.

At first only two, then three and four, and then all the vowels in succession must be so practised:—

A-ye, a-ye-yu, a-ye-yoo-yü, a-ye-yo-yü-yu-yā-yah.

But there must be never more than so much breath at hand as is needed to make the vowel and the tone perfect. The more closely the vowels are connected with the help of the y, the less breath is emitted from the mouth unused, the more intimate is the connection of tone, and the less noticeable are the changes of the position of the organs in relation to each other.

When I pass from yā-yē to yoo, I am compelled to develop very strongly the muscular contraction of the lips, which are formed into a long projecting spout; and this movement cannot be sufficiently exaggerated. With every new y I must produce renewed muscular contractions of the vocal organs, which gradually, through continuous practice, are trained to become almost like the finest, most pliable steel, upon which the fullest reliance may be placed. From yoo it is best to go to yü, that lies still farther forward and requires of the lips an iron firmness; then to yo, touching slightly on the e that lies above the o; then return to yā, and not till then going to ye-ah, which must then feel thus:—

ē

oo-o ah-ā

y

The y is taken under the *ah*, that the word may not slide under; for usually the thought of *ah* relaxes all the organs: the tongue lies flat, the larynx becomes unsteady, is without definite position, and the palate is not arched and is without firmness. In this way *ah* becomes the most colorless and empty vowel of the whole list.

With every change of vowel, or of any other letter, there are changes in the position of the organs, since tongue, palate, and larynx must take different positions for different sounds.

With *ā* and *ē* the larynx stands higher, closer, the palate is sunk, or in its normal position.

With *oo*, *o*, and *ah*, the larynx stands low, the palate is arched.

With *a*, *e*, and *ah* the lips are drawn back.

With *oo*, *o*, *ü*, and *ö* they are extended far forward.

The auxiliary sound y connects them all with each other, so that the transitions are made quite imperceptibly. Since it is pronounced with the tongue drawn high against the palate, it prevents the base of the tongue from falling down again.

This should be practised very slowly, that the sensations may be clearly discerned, and that no vibration that gives the vowel its pitch and duration may escape attention.

The muscular contraction described comprises the chief functions of the vocal organs, and is as necessary for singing as the breath is for the tone. Year in and year out every singer and pupil must practise it in daily exercises as much as possible, on every tone of the vocal compass.

In the lowest as well as in the highest range the sharpness of the *a* is lost, as well as the clear definition of all single vowels. A should be mingled with *oo*, *ah*, and *ē*. In the highest range, the vowels are merged in each other, because then the principal thing is not the vowel, but the high sound.

Even the *thought* of *ā* and *ē*, the latter especially, raises the pitch of the tone. The explanation of this is that *ā* and *ē* possess sympathetic sounds above the palate that lead the breath to the resonance of the head cavities.

For this reason tenors often in high notes resort to the device of changing words with dark vowels to words with the bright vowel *e*. They could attain the same end, without changing the whole word, by simply *thinking* of an *ē*.

Without over-exertion, the singer can practise the exercises given above

I

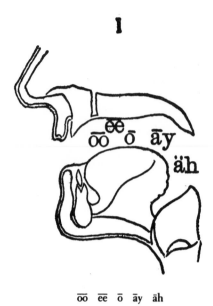

o͞o e͞e ō āy äh

I

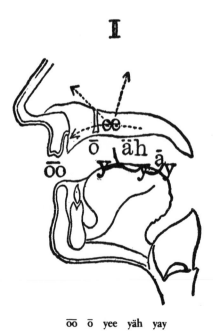

o͞o ō yee yäh yay

twenty times a day, in periods of ten to fifteen minutes each, and will soon appreciate the advantage of the muscular strengthening they give. They make the voice fresh, not weary, as doubtless many will suppose.

What, then, can be expected of an untrained organ? Nothing!

Without daily vocal gymnastics no power of endurance in the muscles can be gained. They must be so strong that a great operatic rôle can be repeated ten times in succession, in order that the singer may become able to endure the strain of singing in opera houses, in great auditoriums, and make himself heard above a great orchestra, without suffering for it.

When I, for instance, was learning the part of *Isolde*, I could without weariness sing the first act alone six times in succession, with expression, action, and a full voice. That was my practice with all my rôles. After I had rehearsed a rôle a thousand times in my own room, I would go into the empty theatre and rehearse single scenes, as well as the whole opera, for hours at a time. That gave me the certainty of being mistress of my resonances down to the last note; and very often I felt able to begin it all over again. So must it be, if one wishes to accomplish anything worth while.

Another end also is attained by the same exercise—the connection, not only of the vowels, but of all letters, syllables, words, and phrases. By this exercise the form for the breath, tone, and word, in which all the organs are adjusted to each other with perfect elasticity, is gradually established. Slowly but surely it assures greatest endurance in all the organs concerned in speaking and singing, the inseparable connection of the palatal resonance with the resonance of the head cavities. In this way is gained perfection in the art of singing, which is based, not on chance, but on knowledge; and this slow but sure way is the only way to gain it.

By the above-described method all other alphabetical sounds can be connected, and exercises can be invented to use with it, which are best adapted to correct the mistakes of pupils, at first on one, then step by step on two and three connected tones, etc.

At the same time it is necessary to learn to move the tongue freely, and with the utmost quickness, by jerking it back, after pronouncing consonants, as quick as a flash, into the position in which we are sure it conducts the breath to the resonating chambers for the vowels, but not before we have disconnected it after pronouncing consonants, which is the same as relaxing the entire form. With all these movements is connected the power of elastically contracting and relaxing the muscles of the tongue and the larynx.

The Lips as a Means of Expression

OF special importance for the tone and the word are the movements of the lips, which are so widely different in the bright and in the dark vowels. These movements cannot be too much exaggerated in practising. The same strength and elasticity to which we have to train the muscles of the throat and tongue must be imparted to the lips, which must be as of iron. Upon their coöperation much of the life of the tone depends, and it can be used in many shadings, as soon as one is able to exert their power consciously and under the control of the will.

Every vowel, every word, every tone, can be colored as by magic in all sorts of ways by the well-controlled play of the lips; can, as it were, be imbued with life, as the lips open or close more or less in different positions. The lips are the final cup-shaped resonators through which the tone has to pass. They can retard it or let it escape, can color it bright or dark, and exert a ceaseless and ever varying influence upon it long before it ceases and up to its very end.

No attempt should be made to use the play of the lips until complete mastery of the absolutely even, perfect tone, and of the muscular powers, has been acquired. The effect must be produced as a result of power and practice; and should not be practised as an effect *per se*.

The Vowel-Sound *AH* of Former Days

THERE is much discussion as to whether *ah*, $\overline{oo}$, or some other vowel is the one best adapted for general practice. In former times practice was entirely on the vowel-sound *ah*. The old Italians taught it; my mother was trained so, and never allowed her pupils to use any other vowel during the first months of their instruction. Later, to be sure, every letter, every word, was practised and improved continually, till it was correct, and had impressed itself upon the memory, as well as the ear, of the pupil for all time.

I explain the matter thus:—

The singer's mouth should always make an agreeable impression. Faces that are forever grinning or showing fish mouths are disgusting and wrong.

The pleasing expression of the mouth requires the muscular contractions that form the bright vowel *ah*.

Most people who are not accustomed to using their vocal resonance pronounce the *ah* quite flat, as if it were the vowel-sound lying lowest. If it is pronounced with the position of the mouth belonging to the bright vowels, it has to seek its resonance, in speaking as well as in singing, in the same place as the dark vowels, on the high-arched palate. To permit this, it must be mingled with $\overline{oo}$. Special attention must be given that the back of the tongue does not fall, but remains high, as in pronouncing *ā*. In this way *ah* comes to lie between $\overline{oo}$-*o'ah'yā*, and forms at the same time the connection between the bright and the dark vowels, and the reverse.

For this reason it was proper that *ah* should be preferred as the practice vowel, as soon as it was placed properly between the two extremes, and had satisfied all demands. It is the most difficult vowel. If it is well pronounced, or sung, it produces the necessary muscular contractions with a pleasing expression of the mouth, and makes certain a fine tone color by its connection with $\overline{oo}$ and o. If the *ah* is equally well formed in all ranges of the voice, a chief difficulty is mastered.

Those, however, who have been badly taught, or have fallen into bad ways, should practise the vocal exercise I have given above, with *yā-yē-yah*, etc., slowly, listening to themselves carefully. Good results cannot fail; it is an infallible means of improvement.

Italians who sing well never speak or sing the vowel sound *ah* otherwise than mixed, and only the neglect of this mixture could have brought about the decadence of the Italian teaching of song. In Germany no attention is paid to it. The *ah*, as sung often by most Italians of the present day, quite flat, sounds commonplace, almost like an affront. It can range itself, that is, connect itself, with no other vowel, makes all vocal connection impossible, evolves very ugly registers, and, lying low in the throat, summons forth no palatal resonance. The power of contraction of the muscles of speech is insufficient, and this insufficiency misleads the singer to constrict the throat muscles, which are not trained to the endurance of it, and thereby further progress is made impossible. In the course of time the tone becomes flat at the transitions. The fatal tremolo is almost always the result of this manner of singing.

Try to sing a scale upward on *ah*, placing the tongue and muscles of speech at the same time on $\bar{a}$, and you will be surprised at the agreeable effect. Even the thought of it alone is often enough, because the tongue involuntarily takes the position of its own accord.

I remember very well how Mme. Desirée Artôt-Padilla, who had a low mezzo-soprano voice, used to toss off great coloratura pieces, beginning on the vowel-sound *ah*, and then going up and down on $\bar{a}$, *ee*, $\bar{a}$*üoah*. At the time I could not understand why she did it; now I know perfectly— because it was easier for her. The breath is impelled against the cavities of the head, the head tones are set into action.

Behind the $\bar{a}$ position there must be as much room provided as is needed for all the vowels, with such modifications as each one requires for itself. The matter of chief importance is the position of the tongue *in* the throat, that it shall not be in the way of the larynx, which must be able to move up and down, even though very slightly, without hindrance.

All vowels must be able to flow into each other; the singer must be able to pass from one to another without perceptible alteration, and back again.

Italian and German

HOW easy it is for the Italians, who have by nature, through the characteristics of their native language, all these things which others must gain by long years of practice! A single syllable often unites three vowels; for instance, "tuoi" (tuoyē), "miei" (myeayē) "muoja," etc.

The Italians mingle all their vowels. They rub them into and color them with each other. This includes a great portion of the art of song, which in every language, with due regard to its peculiar characteristics, must be learned by practice.

To give only a single example of the difficulty of the German words, with the everlasting consonant endings to the syllables, takes the recitative at the entrance of *Norma*:

"Wer lässt hier Aufruhrstimmen, Kriegsruf ertönen, wollt Ihr die Götter zwingen, Eurem Wahnwitz zu fröhnen? Wer wagt vermessen, gleich der Prophetin der Zukunft Nacht zu lichten, wollt Ihr der Götter Plan vorschnell vernichten? Nicht Menschenkräfte können die Wirren dieses Landes schlichten."

Twelve endings on *n*!

"Sediziosi voci, voci di guerra, avvi chi alzar si attenta presso all'ara del Dio? V'ha chi presume dettar responsi alla veggente Norma, e di Roma affrettar il fato arcano? Ei non dipende, no, non dipende da potere umano!"

From the Italians we can learn the connection of the vowels, from the French the use of the nasal tone. The Germans surpass the others in their power of expressiveness. But he who would have the right to call himself an artist must unite all these things; the *bel canto*, that is, beautiful—I might say good—legato-singing, and all the means of expression which we cultivated people need to interpret master works of great minds, should afford the public ennobling pleasure.

A tone full of life depends on the muscular tension of all the vocal organs, on the technical perfection of articulation, as well as on the tone coloring without which it is impossible to attain soulful impression or expression. The larynx must rise and descend unimpeded by the tongue; soft palate and pillars of the fauces rise and sink, the soft palate always able more or less to press close to the hard. Strong and elastic contractions imply very pliable and circumspect relaxation of the same.

The feeling of the extension of the throat comes from the very powerful yet very elastic contraction of the muscles, which, though feeling always in a state of relaxability, appear to me like flexible steel, of which I can demand everything—because never too much—and which I exercise daily. Even in the entr'actes of grand operas I go through with such exercises; for they refresh instead of exhaust me.

The unconstrained coöperation of all the organs, as well as their individual functions, must go on elastically without any pressure or cramped action. Their interplay must be powerful yet supple, that the breath which produces the tone may be diffused as it flows from one to another of the manifold and complicated organs (such as the ventricles of Morgagni), supporting itself on others, being caught in still others, and finding all in such a state of readiness as is required in each range for each tone. Everything must be combined in the right way as a matter of habit.

The voice is equalized by the proper ramification of the breath and the proper connection of the different resonances.

The tone is colored by the proper mixture of vowels; $\overline{oo}$, o, and ah demanding more palatal resonance and a lower position of the larynx, $\bar{a}$ and $\bar{e}$ more resonance of the head cavities and a higher position of the larynx. With $\overline{oo}$, o, $\ddot{u}$, and ah the palate is arched higher (the tongue forming a furrow) than with $\bar{a}$, and $\bar{e}$, where the tongue lies high and flat.

There are singers who place the larynx too low, and, arching the palate too high, sing too much toward $\overline{oo}$. Such voices sound very dark, perhaps even hollow; they lack the interposition of the $\bar{a}$—of the larynx.

On the other hand, there are others who press it upward too high; their $\bar{a}$ position is a permanent one. Such voices are marked by a very bright, sharp quality of tone, often like a goat's bleating.

Both are alike wrong and disagreeable. The proper medium between them must be gained by sensitive training of the ear, and a taste formed by the teacher through examples drawn from his own singing and that of others.

If we wish to give a noble expression to the tone and the word, we must mingle its vocal sound, if it is not $\overline{oo}$, with o or $\overline{oo}$. If we wish to give the word merely an agreeable expression, we mingle it with ah, $\bar{a}$, and $\bar{e}$. That is, we must use all the qualities of tonal resonance, and thus produce colors which shall benefit the tone, and thereby the word and its expression.

Thus a single tone may be taken or sung in many different ways. In every varying connection, consequently, the singer must be able to change it according to the expression desired. But as soon as it is a question of a *musical phrase,* in which several tones or words, or tones alone, are connected, the law of progression must remain in force; expression must be sacrificed, partly at least, to the beauty of the musical passage.

If he is skilful enough, the singer can impart a certain expression of feeling to even the most superficial phrases and coloratura passages. Thus, in the coloratura passages of Mozart's arias, I have always sought to gain expressiveness by *crescendi,* choice of significant points for breathing, and breaking off of phrases. I have been especially successful with this in the "Entführung," introducing a tone of lament into the first aria, an heroic dignity into the second, through the coloratura passages. Without exaggerating petty details, the artist must exploit all the means of expression that he is justified in using.

Auxiliary Vowels

LIKE the auxiliary verbs "will" and "have," $\bar{a}$, $\bar{e}$, and $\overline{oo}$ are auxiliary vowels, of whose aid we are constantly compelled to avail ourselves. It will perhaps sound exaggerated when I present an example of this, but as a matter of fact pronunciation is consummated in this way; only, it must not become noticeable. The method seems singular, but its object is to prevent the leaving of any empty resonance space, and to obviate any interruptions that could affect the perfection of the tone.

For example, when I wish to sing the word "Fräulein," I must first, and before all else, think of the pitch of the tone, before I attack the f. With the f, the tone must be there already, *before* I have pronounced it; to pass from the f to the r I must summon to my aid the auxiliary vowel $\overline{oo}$, or $\bar{a}$ in order to prevent the formation of any unvocalized interstices in the sound. The r must not now drop off, but must in turn be joined to the $\overline{oo}$, while

the tongue should not drop down behind, but should complete the vibrations thus, in a straight line. (See plate.)

It is very interesting to note how much a word can gain or lose in fulness and beauty of tone. Without the use of auxiliary vowels no connection of the resonance in words can be effected; there is then no beautiful tone in singing, only a kind of hacking. Since it must be quite imperceptible, the use of auxiliary vowels must be very artistically managed, and is best practised in the beginning very slowly on single tones and words, then proceeding with great care to two tones, two syllables, and so on. In this way the pupil learns to *hear*. But he must learn to hear very slowly and for a long time, until there is no failure of vibration in the tone and word, and it is all so impressed upon his memory that it can never be lost. The auxiliary vowels must always be present, but the listener should be able to hear, from the assistance of the $\overline{oo}$, only the warmth and nobility of the tone, from the $\bar{a}$ and $\bar{e}$ only the carrying power and brilliancy of it.

Resonant and Disconnected Consonants

K, *l*, *m*, *n*, *p*, *s*, *r*, and *t* at the end of a word or syllable must be made resonant by joining to the end of the word or syllable a rather audible *ĕ*; for instance, Wandell^e, Gretel^e, etc.

A thing that no one teaches any longer, or knows, or is able to do, a thing that only Betz and I knew, and with me will probably disappear entirely, is the dividing and ending of syllables that must be effected under certain conditions. It may have originated with the Italian school.

I was taught it especially upon double consonants. When two come together, they must be divided; the first, as in Him-mel, being sounded dull, and without resonance, the syllable and tone being kept as nasal as possible, the lips closed, and a pause being made between the two syllables; not till then is the second syllable pronounced, with a new formation of the second consonant.

And this is done, not only in case of a doubling of one consonant, but whenever two consonants come together to close the syllable; for instance: win-ter, dring-en, kling-en, bind-en. In these the nasal sound plays a specially important part.

Before articulating *p* and *t* a silent form-pause must be made, because with the *p* the lips are firmly brought together (a vowel cannot be mixed with it), and with *t* the point of the tongue is sharply brought against the hard palate back of the upper teeth, before the abdominal and chest muscles can eject them. *M*, also, may partially be classed with these consonants, since it requires the action of the same muscles, though a lighter shade of vowel coloring may be added. *N* is articulated with *ā*, *ānā*; *r* like *ārrirrā*; the single *s* is softly buzzed like *ssss*; the sibilant *sch* is hissed like *sch-ā* with a narrow opening of the mouth through which while articulating much breath streams directly out. In the case of the German *ch* as in *echt* "the point of contact of the tongue" and palate is placed very far front with *ā* and *ĕ*; when it is combined with dark vowels, as in "doch," "Flucht," "Dach," it is placed farther back with a heightened ōō-palate and the word is articulated far back on the palate with the back of the tongue jammed against it. But if another consonant is placed before the "ch" in words with dark vowels, as in "durch," "Storch," "Furcht," it is classed with the consonants of the lighter front articulation. K is treated like kā, l like ālā. Of all the consonants n is especially an important one. If you wish to convince yourself of the pitch of a note you need only make the trial with n, that is, pronounce ānā and remain long on the n itself with the mouth nearly closed, the lips only being open, and let it ring with a little ē above and a little ā under it. You will learn to sense the nose and the palate exactly, and you will learn to observe how closed everything in the mouth must remain, and how, nevertheless, the chest-sound of the lower resonance as well as the resonance lying above the palate are developed. This high resonance above the palate must ring with every consonant, with every letter. This is, for the properly placed closed vowel (which must not be opened after any consonant, never be sung with the mouth wide open), a guidance for the chest-sound as well as for the high-ringing sound of the note above the palate, taking for granted that during the placement of the tone and during articulation of the word, larynx, chest, and diaphragm coöperate and continue to do so.

The tediousness of singing without proper separation of the syllables is not appreciated till it has been learned how to divide the consonants. The nasal close of itself brings a new color into the singing, which must be taken into account; and moreover, the word is much more clearly intelligible, especially in large auditoriums, where an appreciable length of time is needed for it to reach the listener. By the nasal close, also, an uninterrupted connection is assured between the consonant and the tone, even if the latter has to cease, apparently, for an instant.

I teach all my pupils thus. But since most of them consider it something unheard of to be forced to pronounce in this way, they very rarely bring it to the artistic perfection which alone can make it effective. Except from Betz, I have never heard it from any one. After me no one will teach it any more. I shall probably be the last one. A pity!

Practical Exercises

THE practical study of singing is best begun with single sustained tones, and with preparation on the sound of *ah* alone, mingled with *o* and $\overline{oo}$. A position as if one were about to yawn helps the tongue to lie in the right place.

In order not to weary young voices too much, it is best to begin in the middle range, going upward first, by semitones, and then, starting again with the same tone, going downward. All other exercises begin in the lower range and go upward.

The pupil must first be able to make a single tone good, and judge it correctly before he should be allowed to proceed to a second. Later, single syllables or words can be used as exercises for this.

The position of the mouth and tongue must be watched in the mirror. The vowel *ah* must be mingled with *ō* and $\overline{oo}$, and care must be taken that the breath is forced strongly against the chest, and felt attacking here and on the palate at the same time. Begin *piano*, make a *decrescendo*, then a *crescendo* slowly, and gradually return and end on a well-controlled *piano*.

At the same instant that I place the tone *under* its highest point on the palate, I let the overtones soar above the palate—the two united in one thought. Only in the lowest range can the overtones, and in the highest range the undertones (resonance of the head cavities and of the palate), be dispensed with.

With me the throat never comes into consideration; I feel absolutely nothing of it, at most only the breath gently streaming through it. A tone should never be forced; *never press* the breath against the resonating chambers, but only against the chest; and never hold it back. The abdomen must always be relaxed, let loose, especially when a rapid change of words must be effected. The organs should not be cramped, but should be allowed to perform their functions elastically.

The contraction of the muscles should never exceed their power to relax. A tone must always be sung, whether strong or soft, with an easy, conscious power. Further, before all things, sing always with due regard to the pitch.

In this way the control of the ear is exercised over the pitch, strength, and duration of the tone, and over the singer's strength and weakness, of which we are often forced to make a virtue. In short, one learns to recognize and to produce a perfect tone.

In all exercises go as low and as high as the voice will allow without straining, and always make little pauses to rest between them, even if you are not tired, in order to be all the fresher for the next one. With a certain amount of skill and steady purpose the voice increases its compass, and takes the proper range, easiest to it by nature. The pupil can see then how greatly the compass of a voice can be extended. For amateurs it is not necessary; but it is for every one who practises the profession of a singer in public.

For a second exercise, sing connectedly two half-tones, slowly, on one or two vowels, bridging them with the auxiliary vowels and the y as the support of the tongue, etc.

Every tone must seek its best results from all the organs concerned in its production; must possess power, brilliancy, and mellowness in order to be able to produce, before leaving each tone, the propagation form for the next tone, ascending as well as descending, and make it certain.

No exercise should be dropped till every vibration of every tone has clearly approved itself to the ear, not only of the teacher, but also of the pupil, as *perfect*.

It takes a long time to reach the full consciousness of a tone. After it has passed the lips it must be diffused outside, before it can come to the consciousness of the listener as well as to that of the singer himself. So practise *singing* slowly and *hearing* slowly.

The Great Scale

THIS is the most necessary exercise for all kinds of voices. It was taught to my mother; she taught it to all her pupils and to us. But I am probably the only one of them all who practises it faithfully! I do not trust the others. As a pupil one must practise it twice a day, as a professional singer at least once.

The breath must be well prepared, the expiration still better, for the duration of these five and four long tones is greater than would be supposed.

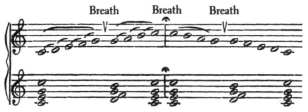

The first tone is positively attacked and by the relaxation of the diaphragm immediately after the attack, is diminished, that is, it is made supple, as the breath is then decreased. All the other vocal organs take up this relaxation and so become elastic. The so-controlled breath may now completely fill up its tone-form as long and as strong as one wishes to make the tone. Yet an excessive *crescendo* is ugly and inartistic. It is due to the energy transformed into elasticity which the attack requires, that a pushing of the breath and a rigid contraction of the organs need not be feared any longer. But one must always remember to make the organ, nose, palate, tongue, larynx, and diaphragm, after every energetic attack, pliable and elastic by relaxing the diaphragm. Then without particularly swelling the tone, that is, making a crescendo, the singer must try, in order to progress, to mentally shape the propagation form for the next

tone. The thought must precede the act a long time. After having fixed
the pitch, the diaphragm and with it all the other organs are again relaxed
and so forced to be pliable. Without altering the form—which insures to
the sustained tone its existence to the last moment—lift nose, palate, and
tongue, with the thoughts dwelling on $\bar{e}$ and $\bar{a}$, and push the new form,
already mentally changed, with an energetic but elastic $\bar{a}$ position of the
larynx in a place created for the next tone. If the pitch which unites $\bar{e}$ and
$\bar{a}$ is secured, then the larynx places itself immediately under the tongue
on $\overline{oo}$, that is, it becomes pliable for new and elastic processes. Now only

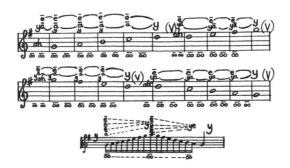

can the second tone also become perfect. Before and after every change of
tone and letter all the mentioned processes are renewed.

The lowest tone must already be prepared to favor the resonance of the
head cavities, that is, the head voice.

It is possible, when $\bar{e}$ is already placed very high, to proceed on $\overline{oo}$.
That would mean to help with the diaphragm, or when the diaphragm
and larynx are already very elastically united on $\overline{oo}$, to proceed on $\bar{e}$, or on
$\bar{e}$ and $\bar{a}$, which would mean to further the progressive motion and change
of tone-form by means of the nose, palate, and tongue.

The larynx adjustment $\bar{a}$ closely connected to the nose position $\bar{e}$,
which also results each time in the relifting of the epiglottis, is and
remains the substance of the tone. By means of it occurs the shifting of
the form toward the top and toward the bottom, an action which unites to
a central point the tones and the positions of the organs, but which
without the y—the elastic hinge—would not bring about a connection in
the tone-progression nor between the relaxation of the old form and the
creation of the new. It is really only a tone-centre. But this focal point
must, in an elastic state, be of service to every form-movement, and may
in cases where the nose, palate, tongue, or diaphragm operate less actively,
be made use of more energetically than would otherwise be necessary in a

normal state. It would mean to give stronger expression to $\bar{a}$ than to $\bar{e}$ or $\overline{oo}$.

There are many singers who produce velocity solely with $\bar{a}$, with a wabbling larynx which acts alone, disunited to nose, palate, or diaphragm. Their tones instead of being connected one with the other, as with a band, tumble out singly. This sort of coloratura, which we used to jokingly call "cluckeratura," is wretched and has nothing in common with the art of song.

When $\overline{oo}$, $\bar{a}$, and $\bar{e}$ are auxiliary vowels, they need not be plainly pronounced. (They form an exception in the diphthongs, "Trauuum," "Leiiid," "Lauuune," "Feuyer," etc.) As auxiliary vowels they are only means to an end, a bridge, a connection from one thing to another. They can be taken anywhere with any other sound; and thence it may be seen how elastic the organs can be when they are skilfully managed.

The chief object of the great scale is to secure the pliant form and the sustained use of the decreasing breath; precision in the preparation of the propagation form; the proper mixture of the vowels which aid in placing the organs in the right position for the tone, to be changed, though imperceptibly, for every different tone; and further, the intelligent use of the resonance of the palate and head cavities, especially the latter, whose tones, soaring above everything else, form the connection with the nasal quality for the whole scale.

The scale must be practised without too strenuous exertion, but not without energy, gradually extending over the entire compass of the voice; and that is, if it is to be perfect, over a compass of two octaves. These two octaves will have been covered, when, advancing the starting-point by semitones, the scale has been carried up through an entire octave. So much every voice can finally accomplish, even if the high notes must be very feeble.

The great scale, properly elaborated in practice, accomplishes wonders: it equalizes the voice, makes it flexible and noble, gives strength to all weak places, operates to repair all faults and breaks that exist, and controls the voice to the very heart. Nothing escapes it.

Its use brings ability as well as inability to light—something that is extremely unpleasant to those without ability. In my opinion it is the ideal exercise, but the most difficult one I know. By devoting forty minutes to it every day, a consciousness of certainty and strength will be gained that ten hours a day of any other exercise cannot give.

This should be the chief test in all conservatories. If I were at the head of one, the pupils should be allowed for the first three years to sing at the examinations only *difficult* exercises, like this great scale, before they should be allowed to think of singing a song or an aria, which I regard only as cloaks for incompetency.

For teaching me this scale—this guardian angel of the voice—I cannot be thankful enough to my mother. In earlier years I used to like to shirk the work of singing it. There was a time when I imagined that it strained me. My mother often ended her warnings at my neglect of it with the words, "You will be very sorry for it!" And I was very sorry for it. At one time, when I was about to be subjected to great exertions, and did not practise it every day, but thought it was enough to sing coloratura fireworks, I soon became aware that my transition tones would no longer endure the strain, began easily to waver, or threatened even to become too flat. The realization of it was terrible! It cost me many, many years of the hardest and most careful study; and it finally brought me to realize the necessity of exercising the vocal organs continually, and in the proper way, if I wished always to be able to rely on them.

Practice, and especially the practice of the great, slow scale, is the only cure for all injuries, and at the same time the most excellent means of fortification against all over-exertion. I sing it every day, often twice, even if I have to sing one of the greatest rôles in the evening. I can rely absolutely on its assistance.

If I had imparted nothing else to my pupils but the ability to sing this one great exercise well, they would possess a capital fund of knowledge which must infallibly bring them a rich return on their voices. I often take fifty minutes to go through it only once, for I let no tone pass that is lacking in any degree in pitch, power, and duration, or in a single vibration of the propagation form.

Velocity

SINGERS, male and female, who are lacking velocity and the power of trilling, seem to me like horses without tails. Both of these things belong to the art of song, and are inseparable from it. It is a matter of indifference whether the singer has to use them or not; he must be able to. The teacher who neither teaches nor can teach them to his pupils is a *bad teacher*; the pupil who, notwithstanding the urgent warnings of his teacher, neglects the exercises that can help him to acquire them, and fails to perfect himself in them, is a *bungler*. There is no excuse for it but lack of talent, or laziness; and neither has any place in the higher walks of art.

Those also must be condemned who have so-called faults in articulation due generally to a lazy tongue. I refer to those who lisp because their tongue remains fastened to the point of contact on the upper teeth, when articulating *s*, *sh*, or *z*. I sentence them to death as far as the art of song is concerned.

To give velocity, practise first slowly, then faster and faster figures of five, six, seven, and eight notes, etc., upward and downward.

If one has well mastered the great, slow scale, with the nasal connection, skill in singing rapid passages will be developed quite of itself, because they both rest on the same foundation, and without the preliminary practice can never be understood.

Place the palate in a nasal position, the larynx and tongue on *āyē*, tense the chest muscles and diaphragm toward each other, and attack the lowest tone on the height of the highest tone of the figure. Force the breath toward the chest muscles by vigorously articulating toward the chest without losing entirely the nasal position and run up the scale with great firmness and tension while thinking the larynx as downward in front.

In descending keep the form of the highest tone be the descent ever so long; place *āyē* still closer to each other and toward the nose, so that the scale slides down not a pair of stairs but a smooth track in an upward direction, the highest tone affording, as it were, a guarantee that on the way there shall be no impediment or sudden drop. The resonance form, kept firm and tense, must by means of the elasticity of the organs adapt itself with the utmost freedom to the thought of every tone, and with it, to the breath. The pressure of the breath against the chest must not be diminished but must be unceasing.

It must always be as if the pitch of the highest tone were already contained in the lowest, so strongly concentrated upon the whole figure are my thoughts at the attack of a single tone. By means of $\bar{e}$-$\bar{a}$-$\overline{oo}$, larynx, tongue, and palatal position on the lowest tone are in such a position that the vibrations of breath for the highest tones are already finding admission into the head cavities.

The higher and more brilliant the vocal figures go, the more breath they need. But because there is a limit to the scope of the movement of larynx and tongue, and they cannot rise higher, the singer must resort to the aid of the auxiliary vowel $\overline{oo}$, in order to lower the larynx.

A run or any other figure must never sound thus:

but must be nasally modified above, and tied; and because the breath must flow out unceasingly in a powerful stream from the vocal cords, an *h* can only be put in beneath, which makes us sure of this powerful streaming out of the breath, and helps only the branch stream of breath into the cavities of the head. Often singers hold the breath, concentrated on the nasal form, firmly on the lowest tone of a figure, and, without interrupting this nasal form, or the head tones, that is, the breath vibrating in the head cavities, finish the figure alone. When this happens the muscular contractions of the throat, tongue, and palate are very strong, that is, the breath pressure becomes rigid, and the decreasing breath performs the work alone.

The turn, too, is based on the consistent connection of the tonal figure with the nasal quality and the diaphragm, which is obtained by pronouncing the o͞o toward the nose, by means of which the larynx is made pliable. The *y* insures the connection of all vowels to one another; it is the mobile hinge of the closed form. Every vowel is ready to help—for ascending *ā*

L'oiselet   Chopin-Viardot

and *ē*, for descending o͞o. In the closed form they accomplish the change of form quickly and elastically without ever relaxing it entirely.

With combined strength, especially with the cooperation of one or the other organ, numberless nuances may be attained through conscious practice in the *piano*, in the *forte*, in *messa di voce*, in darker or lighter coloring, in the velocity or breadth of the form, with one breath. In such manner every one can attain velocity, and if he is apt, apply it in serious song.

How often have I heard the ha-ha-ha-haa, etc.—a wretched tumbling down of different tones, instead of a smooth decoration of the cantilena. Singers generally disregard it, because no one can do it any more, and yet even to-day it is of the greatest importance. (See "Tristan und Isolde.")

The situation is quite the same in regard to the appoggiatura. In this the resonance is made nasal without losing the connection with the diaphragm. The flexibility of the larynx—which, without changing the resonance, moves quickly up and down—accomplishes the task alone. Here, too, it can almost be imagined that the *thought* alone is enough, for the connection of the two tones cannot be too close. But this must be practised, and done *consciously*.

Adelaide, by Beethoven

A-   bend-lüft-chen   im   zar-ten   Lau-be   flü-stern

Trill

THERE still remains the trill, which is best practised in the beginning as follows—always from the upper note to the lower one:

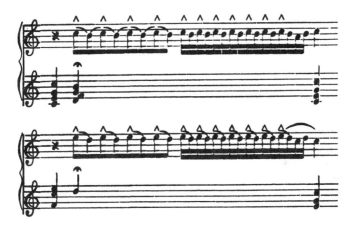

ā and *ē* are placed very closely against each other, nearly pinching, and held tight; the larynx kept as stiff as possible and placed high. Both tones are connected as closely, as heavily as possible, upward nasally, downward *on* the larynx, for which the *y*, again, is admirably suited. They must be attacked as high as possible, and very strongly connected with the chest and diaphragm. The trill exercise must be practised almost as a scream. The upper note must always be strongly *accented*. The exercise is practised with an even strength, without decrescendo to the end; the breath pressure and articulation act more and more strongly, uninterruptedly to the finish.

Trill exercises must be performed with great energy, on the whole compass of the voice. They form an exception to the rule in so far that in them more is given to the throat to do—always, however, under the control of the chest and the diaphragm—than in other exercises. That relates, however, to the muscles.

The breath vibrates *above* the larynx, but does not stick in it, consequently this is not dangerous. It is really a gymnastic exercise for the muscles.

The exercise is practised first on two half, then on two whole, tones of the same key (as given above), advancing by semitones, twice a day on the entire compass of the voice. It is exhausting because it requires great energy; but for the same reason it gives strength. Practise it first as slowly and vigorously as the strength of the throat allows, then faster and faster, till one day the trill unexpectedly appears. With some energy and industry good results should be reached in from six to eight weeks, and the larynx should take on the habit of performing its function by itself, so that it seems as if only *one* tone were attacked and held, and as if the second tone simply vibrated with it. As a matter of fact, the larynx will have been so practised in the minute upward-and-downward motion, that the singer is aware only of the vibrations of the breath that lie *above* it.

The technique for it is the following: After the correct slow and quick practice of the above exercise, the lower tone only is held with the larynx by means of the vowel $\bar{a}$ and connected with the chest and diaphragm muscles. The upper tone remains over it in the nasal form, which becomes stronger and more concentrated as soon as the lower tone is attacked. Then the lower tone, which is placed yet higher, attacks very strongly and closely the upper one with the ever renewed $\bar{a}$. The upper tone vibrates with it through the acquired habit taken by the larynx and through the memory. One has the feeling, then, as singing or holding only the lower tone (placed and sung exceedingly high) while the upper tone vibrates with it through the habit of accentuation. The union of the two then comes to the singer's consciousness as if he were singing the lower note somewhat too high, halfway toward the upper one. This is only an aural delusion, produced by the high vibrations. But the trill, when fully mastered, should always be begun, as in the exercise, on the *upper* note.

Every voice must master the trill, after a period, longer or shorter, of proper practice. Stiff, strong voices master it sooner than small, weak ones. I expended certainly ten years upon improving it, because as a young girl I had so very little strength, although my voice was very flexible in executing all sorts of rapid passages.

To be able to use it anywhere, of course, requires a long time and much practice. For this reason it is a good plan to practise it on syllables with different vowels, such as can all be supported on $\bar{a}$ and $\bar{e}$, and on words, as soon as the understanding needed for this is in some degree assured.

If the larynx has acquired the habit properly, the trill may be led, by decreasing the breath, from *piano* to *pianissimo* and, through the control of the breath pressure and a firmer articulation of $\bar{a}$ and $\bar{e}$, be prolonged almost without end with crescendi and decrescendi, as the old Italians used to do and as all German singers do who have learned something.

How to Hold One's Self when Practising

In practising the singer should always stand, if possible, before a large mirror, in order to be able to watch himself closely. He should stand upright, quietly but not stiffly, and avoid everything that looks like restlessness. The hands should hang quietly, or rest lightly on something, without taking part as yet in the interpretation of the expression. The first thing needed is to bring the body under control, that is, to remain quiet, so that later, in singing, the singer can do everything intentionally.

The pupil must always stand in such a way that the teacher can watch his face, as well as his whole body. Continual movements of the fingers, hands, or feet are not permissible.

The body must serve the singer's purposes freely and must acquire no bad habits. The singer's self-possession is reflected in a feeling of satisfaction on the part of the listener. The quieter the singer or artist, the more significant is every expression he gives; the fewer motions he makes the more importance they have. So he can scarcely be quiet enough. Only there must be a certain accent of expression in this quietude, which cannot be represented by indifference. The quietude of the artist is a reassurance for the public, for it can come only from the certainty of power and the full command of his task through study and preparation and perfect knowledge of the work to be presented. An artist whose art is based on power cannot appear other than self-possessed and certain of himself. An evident uneasiness is always inartistic, and hence does not belong where art is to be embodied. All dependence upon tricks of habit creates nervousness and lack of flexibility.

Therefore the singer must accustom himself to quietude in practising, and make his will master of his whole body, that later he may have free command of all his movements and means of expression.

The constant playing of single tones or chords on the piano by the teacher during the lesson is wrong, and every pupil should request its discontinuance. The teacher can hear the pupil, but the latter cannot hear himself, when this is done; and yet it is of the utmost importance that he should learn to hear himself. I am almost driven distracted when teachers bring me their pupils, and drum on the piano as if possessed while they sing. Pupils have the same effect on me when they sit and play a dozen chords to one long note.

Do they sit in the evening when they sing in a concert?

Do they hear themselves, when they do this?—I cannot hear them.

Poor pupils!

It is enough for a musical person to strike a single note on the piano when he practises alone, or perhaps a common chord, after which the body and hands should return to their quiet, natural position. Only in a standing posture can a free, deep breath be drawn, and mind and body be properly prepared for the exercise or the song to follow.

It is also well for pupils to form sentences with the proper number of syllables upon which to sing their exercises, so that even such exercises shall gradually gain a certain amount of expressiveness. Thus the exercises will form pictures which must be connected with the play of the features, as well as with an inner feeling, and thus will not become desultory and soulless and given over to indifference. Of course not till the mere tone itself is brought under complete control, and uncertainty is no longer possible, can the horizon of the pupil be thus widened without danger.

Only when a scene requires that a vocal passage be sung kneeling or sitting must the singer practise it in his room long before the performance and at all rehearsals, in accordance with dramatic requirements of the situation. *Otherwise the singer should always* STAND. We must also look out for unaccustomed garments that may be required on the stage, and rehearse in them; for instance, hat, helmet, hood, cloak, etc. Without becoming accustomed to them by practice, the singer may easily make himself ridiculous on the stage. Hence comes the absurdity of a Lohengrin who cannot sing with a helmet, another who cannot with a shield, a third who cannot with gauntlets; a Wanderer who cannot with the big hat, another who cannot with the spear, a José who cannot with the helmet, etc. All these things must be practised before a mirror until the requirements of a part or its costume become a habit. To attain this, the singer must be completely master of his body and all his movements.

It must be precisely the same with the voice. The singer must be quite independent of bad habits in order consciously to exact from it what the proper interpretation of the work to be performed requires.

He should practise only so long as can be done without weariness. After every exercise he should take a rest, to be fresh for the next one. After the great scale he should rest *at least* ten minutes; and these resting times must be observed as long as one sings, and not be filled with other tasks.

Long-continued exertion should not be exacted of the voice at first; even if the effects of it are not immediately felt, a damage is done in some way. In this matter pupils themselves are chiefly at fault, because they cannot get enough, as long as they take pleasure in it.

For this reason it is insane folly to try to sing important rôles on the stage after one or two years of study; it may perhaps be endured for one or two years without evil results, but it can never be carried on indefinitely.

Agents and managers commit a crime when they demand enormous exertions of such young singers. The rehearsals, which are held in abominably bad air, the late hours, the irregular life that is occasioned by rehearsals, the strain of standing around for five or six hours in a theatre, all this is not for untrained young persons. No woman of less than twenty-four years should sing soubrette parts, none of less than twenty-eight years second parts, and none of less than thirty-five years dramatic parts; that is early enough. By that time proper preparation can be made, and in voice and person something can be offered worth while. And our fraternity must realize this sooner or later. In that way, too, they will learn more and be able to do more, and fewer sins will be committed against the art of song by the incompetent.

Pronunciation—Consonants

WITHOUT doubt the Italian language with its wealth of vowels is better adapted for singing than the German language so rich in consonants, or than any other language. The organs of speech and the vocal apparatus, in the Italian language, are less subjected to violent form-modifications. The numerous vowels secure for the singer an easy connection of the sounds, while the poor pronunciation of the many hard consonants interrupts every form- and tone-connection. However, every one who professes to be an artist should learn to pronounce and sing well every current language. The mixing and connecting of several vowels in the different vowel-forms on single tones is a study in itself. The most appropriate exercise for it consists in placing a y before each vowel and of renewing it before each following vowel, so that y becomes a binding medium and at the same time a gymnastic exercise for the muscles of the vocal apparatus.

First sing one or two syllables very slowly in one breath, so as to learn to observe each vibration and each position of the tongue and the palate; then gradually add a third and a fourth syllable. The y is so slowly prepared by the tongue that it seems like a syllable itself.

If we take into consideration that many German words contain as many consonants as vowels, which must be pronounced and resonate on a single tone, as for example, Sprung, Strauch, bringst, Herbst, schweifst, brauchst, etc., we must acquire great deftness of the vocal apparatus, that is, with the tongue, larynx, palate, lips, nose, chest, and diaphragm, so that we can at least approximately meet such great demands. To begin with, we must try clearly to understand that every letter demands its own form, that every union of the vocal organs from one letter or tone to another must again create a new form. Perhaps it is better to say in this instance: a new quality of the form or tone. In order to accomplish this the existing form must in its concentration be resolved into y—which prevents the form from falling apart—before a change can be made to a new form, that is, a new position, no matter whether a tone, vowel, or consonant, or an entire word is to be changed. Each of the three first mentioned form-modifications has its own particular quality. If several of them take place simultaneously, the change will be doubly difficult.

Dark vowels are to be thought of as concave, bright vowels as straight, and consonants as convex.

Dark vowels ⌣, bright vowels ═══, consonants ⌢ .

All vowels, all consonants need auxiliary vowels. A vowel by itself with its finest shades of tone-color is impossible. The bright $\bar{a}$ and $\bar{e}$ would

sound shrill and not strong enough, and the dark $\overline{oo}$ and $\bar{o}$ would sound hollow, if not a mixture of dark and bright respectively, which in this case would denote body and pitch of tone, were added.

As we see, the vowel *ah* is composed of three other vowels, $\bar{e}$, $\bar{a}$, $\overline{oo}$. These three vowels connected by *y* enclose a small space in which they are transformed into a fourth. It is left to the singer's taste to make the fourth vowel bright with $\bar{e}$ stronger with the aid of $\bar{a}$, and darker and more covered with the aid of $\overline{oo}$. The $\bar{e}$ at the nose gives tone-height, the $\bar{a}$ position of the tongue transfers strength to the larynx and its many muscles and cartilages; the $\overline{oo}$ lifts the back of the tongue toward the nose and at the same time gives it the sonorous depth which a perfect tone requires. By means of $\overline{oo}$ the larynx takes a low position, is made supple, and is prepared for the form-modifications.

To prevent extreme differences in sounds from bright to dark or vice versa, the two forms in the pronunciation of the word must be brought as near together as possible, *e.g.* the vowels must be colored or mixed according to the warmth and character of the word to be sung. As consonants compress all vowel-forms and so cut off all tone-connection, we are compelled to look for a means to preserve sound- and tone-connection. It consists in pronouncing nearly all consonants in the $\bar{a}$ form and during the enunciation in altering the concave and convex positions often, so that a kind of wavelike motion is produced in which the consonants may often resound with the vowel, as for example:

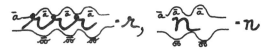

The process is particularly noticeable with *r*. But *s*, *m*, *l*, *d*, though pronounced in a different manner, also need all auxiliary vowels. While several vowels are always adjusted to sound as one, the consonants must, during the process of articulation, be slowly produced by the flexible motion and counter-motion of larynx, tongue and palate, chest and diaphragm. During their formation and even in their preparation they take up considerable time, as they have to perform a twofold work in order to resound. It is then the exact opposite to that which most singers and pupils understand by clear-cut and correct articulation, or to that which they are in the habit of doing by giving the consonants a hard, quick, and toneless articulation without preparing them and without making them flexible.

With most consonants it is a question of the vowel-form $\bar{a}$ in which they are placed and articulated, as the vowel $\bar{a}$ must nearly always be pronounced before a word and generally after a word closing with a consonant. In the latter case it is used as a sort of after-sound, for example:

If in addition there is a question of pitch, then even $\bar{a}$, the note-line (with which I have underlined the word), is not sufficient. There must be added to the $\bar{a}$ an $\bar{e}$ over the nose, that is, the $\bar{a}$ must be placed higher. Prefixes and suffixes as in "verraten," "verleugnen," "zertrümmern," etc., receive a covering of $\overline{oo}$ or $\ddot{o}$, treating them as if they were written without $\bar{e}$—thus—vörratönö. In this way they become secondary to the main

syllable which, especially in the recitative, cannot be too strongly accented.

We see how, in defiance to all the opposition which the consonants are ever ready to offer the vocal apparatus of the singer or speaker, the modified concave vocal form remains victorious. It remains victorious as long as the distinctness of the consonant is only attained through the coresonance of the bright vowels $\bar{a}$, $\bar{e}$, and often also through the coresonance of $\overline{oo}$ and $\ddot{o}$.

All singing, and especially the consonants, requires the $\bar{a}$ position of the tongue; for example: (The sign ⌢ denotes silent preparation.)

$$\hat{\bar{a}}\ b\ \bar{a}, \hat{\bar{a}}\ c\ \bar{a}, \hat{\bar{a}}\ d\ \bar{a}, \hat{\bar{a}}f\ \bar{o}f, \hat{\bar{a}}\ g\ a, \hat{\bar{a}}ch\ u, \hat{\bar{a}}j\ \bar{e}, \hat{\bar{a}}\ l\ \bar{a}, \hat{\bar{a}}\ m\ \bar{a},$$

$$\bar{a}\ n\ \bar{a}, \hat{\bar{a}}p\ \bar{a}, \hat{\bar{a}}k\ \bar{e}, \hat{\bar{a}}rr, \overline{ss}, \hat{\bar{a}}t\ \bar{a}, v\ r, \hat{\bar{a}}x, \hat{\bar{a}}tzat\ a$$

It will be said that this is natural. Yes, but no singer gives himself consciously the time to prepare, then to relax, and then to interchange the two widely different actions (motion and counter-motion) as called forth by the comprehensive vowel- and consonant-forms by making the muscles of the entire vocal apparatus pliable; in short, no one gives himself the time to give each letter its sound and its value.

There now presents itself a second art which we may confidently name the art of consonants. Entirely different from the vowel-art and still united to it, it presents to the singer the most difficult task, one with which he has a lifelong struggle without really knowing what it is he has to overcome. He generally looks for the cause in the pronunciation of the vowel, or in the breath, or attack. It is not the vowel, but the preceding or succeeding consonant that constricts the form and prevents the continuance of tonal resonance. In time many singers lose their voice through the inflexibility of the muscles of the tongue and larynx. As beauty of tone is the foundation of vocal art, it should be the aim of every singer to alter it as little as possible by means of skilful and flexible pronunciation without endangering the distinctness of enunciation.

Not only the word and syllable, which are sung in the form of the dominating vowel of the word, but every letter necessitates a form-modification. One letter jeopardizes another, every letter imperils tone-beauty, every consonant endangers every vowel, one form another, in which one must pronounce or sing. Stability, beauty, height, depth, strength, and suppleness of tone and word run eternal danger of being altered and thrown from their path.

In order to equalize the form-modifications it is necessary constantly to employ all those auxiliary vowels—especially $\bar{a}$ and $\bar{e}$—which have the power to raise the tongue and palate, thus raising the pitch and form. Every vowel may eventually be an auxiliary vowel—according to the demands of tone-beauty. We can better see from an illustration what a revolution the change of letters in the form of a perfect tone endeavors to bring about; how the singer must concentrate his entire attention on the form-modifications or form-preservation while articulating every letter so that he may remain master of the beauty of his voice. No letter, no syllable ought to be pronounced badly. The teacher should not let a poorly pronounced syllable pass uncorrected. He must correct over and over again until letter, syllable, and word are connected with each other by good resonance.

As I have often mentioned, we shall have to abolish the false designations used in the pedagogics of vocal art as well as those used by the professional singer—erroneous appellations which produce false comprehension on the part of the teacher and singer—for example: the false idea of the breath on which for years nearly the entire attention was directed, thus diverting it from the form for the breath. The misunderstood idea of breath-restraint (*Atemstauen*) on the part of the pupil corresponds to the idea of a channel without outlet, in which the water collects without flowing off; whereas the breath must continually issue from the mouth. It has become the habit of considering the breath as the only cause for a bad or a good tone. This is the cause of the eternal breath pressure with which so many singers produce their tones and ruin their voices. Tone and tone-strength may be produced only by muscle-stretching and by the subtlest tension of the vocal organs. To avoid such an error it would be advisable to leave the coaction of the diaphragm out of play at first, directing the entire attention to the form only, that is, to the relative position of nose, palate, larynx, and tongue, and finally, after the form has become habit, to the fine, subtle, and dirigible coworker, the diaphragm.

Another false conception is the attack, which one locates in the nose, another in the larynx, a third in the abdomen, a fourth in the brain, etc. As if the attack of a tone depended on a single point! (See section on Attack and on Vowels.) Breath pressure and tightening of the diaphragm, which counteract the relaxation of the upper organs, or any counter-pressure of the diaphragm against these, are gross errors.

Just as grave a mistake takes place when the singer, instead of using the coöperating tensed muscles which hold together the form, leaves the tone (vibrating breath) to the mercy of the formless, that is, the untensed organs. This often and wrongly happens when singing *piano*. Instead of relaxing the entire form, one part into another, he either lets go entirely the diaphragm and tightens the upper organs, or he holds the breath

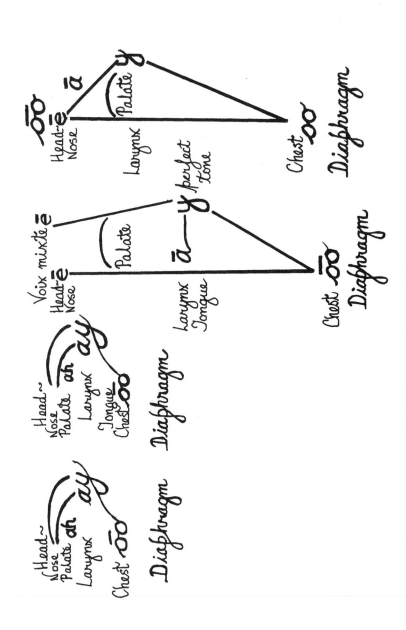

instead of letting it flow flexibly, and dissolves the connection between the diaphragm and the upper organs, which then wabble helplessly to and fro, producing tremolo and uncertainty. I have seen one such tone (breath) left formless, ruin the entire evening for the singer. Because he was suddenly robbed of all support, he thought himself suddenly indisposed and was unable to sing to the end. Unfortunate ignorance! Wretched art!

The weakest as well as the strongest tone which the singer is able to give depends on the energy of the experienced artist, upon the lesser or greater tension of all the muscles of the vocal organs in themselves and one to the other. This tension extends from the nose, the temples, over the larynx, and the chest muscles down to the diaphragm. At certain heights the nose and the diaphragm are the poles from which the tension from one to the other seems like the tensed string of a harp. Without this tension a steady tone is an impossibility. It naturally becomes weaker and more flexible the lower we descend, and more tensed the higher we wish to sing.

In this form, whose ends or poles are tensed against each other, everything takes place which the intervening organs, such as larynx and tongue—which must likewise be in exact tension with them—have to execute in articulating, or which they have to execute in the progression of the tone toward the height or depth. Only he whose ear is so acutely trained that he can hear that each tone interruption is produced by the poor action of larynx and tongue or by the tightening of the diaphragm or soft palate, or by muscular laxness, has any idea of the delicacy of the work; and only he has any idea of it, who through years of work has tried to produce tone-binding in such a manner that the tone will continue to resonate uninterruptedly in spite of the difficulties offered by the language he is using, or by bad and careless habits of speech. That would mean to be moderate; to hold together all organs flexibly but still energetically, not to allow the action of any one organ to predominate, and to avoid anything that would injure the form. The coöperation of the chest muscles—also a tension—which I could almost indicate as an external sensation, is like the auxiliary vowels. We can make use of these muscles in the higher and highest range as soon as the chest voice is to coresonate, that is, as soon as a perfect or nearly perfect tone is to resound. By so doing, the larynx, nearly entirely relieved, is now a sort of balance; that is, the cartilages of the larynx need not accentuate the higher position so firmly that they alone would give the strength. The cartilages are relaxed or supported by the chest muscles, an external sensation.

In addition to this external sensation of the chest muscles, the external muscles of the throat (which extend down to and lose themselves in the chest muscles) take part. I have the feeling as if my throat and larynx were suspended from my temples and with them the tone which is extended simultaneously toward the top and toward the bottom.

To some extent, we here see what resources are at our disposal, and that only by the conscious knowledge of the adjustment of our vocal organs—which must be one with our ear (hearing)—may a permanent art or a lasting voice (within human limits) be secured. The coöperation of all muscles, ligaments, tendons, and nerves with each other, and the action within themselves must be secured to produce a mobile, supple, movable, and indestructible form for the breath. The form may be modified but never destroyed. Some singers have natural gifts. The true artist, though, has worked over them and directed them into artistic paths. We need only to have observed Joseph Kainz (a noted German actor), whose muscular tension and elasticity were admirable and from whose technique of breathing every singer could learn. Such wonderful technique, united with such a wonderful soul as in this case, gave the listener the keenest enjoyment. And surely he could only have acquired this technique through very earnest study, and perhaps through the knowledge that a lasting art is impossible without technique. Also in listening to the concert singer Meschaert you can very well hear the striking elasticity of larynx and palate, which so charmed me in his wonderful singing.

Consciously or unconsciously used, technique remains a necessity to art and to the artist himself, as without it there is no art. Is it not a magnificent task to secure for one's self a privileged position in the world of art by acquiring conscious ability? By gaining for one's self a beautiful voice, if such a one naturally exists, by preserving it to the end of one's life?

Singers have acquired the habit of pronouncing words in the same direction as they are written, that is, from left to right, from front to back; this also gives a false idea of pronunciation in vocal art. Words to be sung artistically are not sung as the majority are in the habit of pronouncing ordinarily; not in a straight line, but in accordance with note-height and depth, beginning almost at the pharynx and placing before the last pronounced letter, letter for letter. Only a few artists have a clear and conscious idea of this. How rarely does any one speak sonorously, and to speak thus would signify to join words constantly, one to the other in vowel forms!

With many German singers and speakers the back and root of the tongue remain rigid in the throat while pronouncing consonants, especially the end consonants of a word. No one, unless he naturally speaks flexibly, thinks of relaxing the form before and after each consonant and of creating new vowel forms for the additional auxiliary vowels which aid in rendering the consonant sonorous and intelligible. For example:

$\bar{a} Naval \bar{a}, \quad \bar{a} Haven \bar{a}, \bar{a} Craven \bar{a}$

Naturally the auxiliary vowel is only a prolongation of sonority and is not an articulated syllable.

K, p, and *t* are toneless consonants and must be prepared in a mute form. When consonants are doubled, as, for example, in

Himmel, Anna, Elle etc.

the first consonant must also be mute and the second only be given a resonant pronunciation. All other consonants are made clear and singable with the aid of auxiliary vowels both in their preparation and in their articulation. This end-form, even if it should be necessary to breathe in between, serves at the same time as a preparatory form for the following word or tone. The elasticity, the tone-generator, and the tone-carrying power are soon lost, when the tongue and root of tongue compel hard and constricted muscular movements in the form instead of elastic ones. Rigidity of the vocal apparatus can, though, be caused by any single organ and very rapidly communicates itself to all other organs from the top down or vice versa, as soon as they are in some degree connected. The thyroid and cricoid cartilages, the two important distributors of strength, are in such instances so compressed that they make everything connected with them immovable. And especially the strength of a tone, which comes into existence by the placement of the larynx (in the $\bar{e}$ and $\overline{oo}$ tension) by means of the vowel $\bar{a}$, whose coworkers are the cricoid and thyroid cartilages (especially in the higher and highest voix-mixte tones), must only be produced in an elastic manner. The cartilages must be drawn together as if by a magnet; they must then be held together elastically, and then be elastically relaxed. As soon as the tongue and root of tongue through stiffness or contraction hinder the action of the cartilages, all the muscles of the larynx become cramped and for the moment the singer is lost.

I can only compare the sensation of this elastic magnetic force to that of two fine magnetic needles—or to two slowly moving bolts in a machine—which are drawn toward each other to a certain point but can never touch each other, and which, notwithstanding the force of attraction, tend to retract. So the placement of the vowel $\bar{a}$ with the larynx—

which now takes a position between two magnetic poles—creates a balance of strength upon which the tone must soaringly be maintained. For example:

Pronunciation that is too distinct, particularly of consonants, destroys all tone-connection and the tone- and propagation-form.

But singing depends chiefly on the connection of tones. Every single tone in a scale, for example, may be right, but the connection from one tone to another very wrong. The error arises from the fact that the form of the tone just completed was not entirely relaxed, and the tension of the organs one to the other was not dissolved before the form was prepared for the next tone. The refined singer must learn to hear this work of connection and dissolution. To complete two tones, then, there are necessary four different though connected forms. The transition form from one tone to another must naturally not be heard and yet the two tones of a scale would lack an important factor if this transition form were not present, which, for example, I not only hear but of which I also have a distinct sensation (when hearing others). The connecting form then is an intermediate form for a mute intermediate sound. It lies between two different tones or letters and is effected principally by the relaxation of the diaphragm and larynx, which extends over the entire form and diminishes the current of breath. It is only when this process (corresponding to the dissolution of the form) is perfectly accomplished, that the entire vocal organs (tensed in themselves and one to the other, making the vocal apparatus) are shifted the entire length for the second tone, toward the top for height and toward the bottom for depth of tone, without disturbing the main form and the stream of breath. The breath is conducted in this progressive form to that place whose position corresponds to the height or depth of the tone which we are about to sing. The thought, the ear (hearing), and the adjustment of the vocal organs must naturally be one! This moving intermediate form is the connecting form from one tone to another, which, as we will see later, is made still more complicated through the pronunciation of words. Without this continual tone-connection there is no cantilena and no vocal art. The pronunciation of consonants exacts a certain distinctness which, however, is not produced by the cramped stiffness of the organs, or by the vigorous expulsion of the consonants. On the contrary, the preparation for them must take place in very pliable vowel-forms whether for sonant or surd consonants, so that the path from vowel to consonant and vice versa is kept resounding and the current of breath is not interrupted.

The voiceless consonants k, p, t are prepared silently but with flexibility. The labials like f and w, the sibilants s, sch, z, the aspirates like ch (German), ph, v (German), whether pronounced with lips, upper teeth, root of tongue and palate, with tip of tongue and protruding underlip, or in any other manner, must according to their peculiarity be intonated *very* slowly (though we can hardly say they are rendered quite sonorous). Nearly all of them are intonated in the $\bar{a}$-form.

CHEMIE: $\bar{a}$ CH$^{ch\bar{e}}$ $^{ch\bar{i}}$ EMIE$^{\bar{e}}$ VORNE: $\bar{a}$ V$_{o}^{o}$ O $\overset{\curvearrowright}{a\bar{a}\bar{a}}$ NE $\bar{a}$

SCHILD: $\bar{a}$ SCH $^{sch\ sh\bar{a}}$ $^{\bar{a}\,\bar{a}}$ ILD   KALT: $\overset{\bar{e}}{\underset{}{K}}$ $\overset{\bar{a}}{\underset{}{A}}$ LT $\bar{a}$

STUMM: $^{\bar{a}}$ SCH $\overset{\frown}{\underline{\underline{oo}}}$ TUMM $\bar{a}$

After each consonant-pause ($\frown$) , which serves as well for distinct utterance as for preparation, the consonant in question, as k, p, t, must be pronounced very distinctly and quickly.

Every letter, vowel, or consonant requires then not only its own distinct form, transition form, and adjustment in regard to tone-height—by adjustment in regard to tone-height is meant the $\bar{a}$-line of concentrated force—but it modifies its own form continually by calling into play other vowels which tend to make the form flexible, to place it higher, to spread it, to make it narrower, in short, everything which tends to change the tonal quality.

According to tone-height and the demands of the word, the modified form moves from one letter to another without altering the note-line $\bar{a}$, the pitch and purity of the tone. Every tone can lay claim to various heights according to the harmony to which it belongs.

To render the necessary form-modifications as comfortable as possible for the vocal apparatus, to adapt them advantageously for the tone-height, and to use them in such a manner that the ear of the listener is insensible to the changes, is the great feat of vocal art. He who expects rapid progress during the study of this most difficult task will never master the art of song. There are endless difficulties to overcome, there are so many words in all languages, there exist so many complications in the sentence arrangement that it becomes a life-long study.

The ignorant, the unskilful, or the careless will easily cramp his organs in making the rapid modifications of the form. If this becomes habit, the singer is to be pitied, for, as grand as his profession could be, it now becomes a torture. To prevent this, he must become acquainted with his vocal apparatus with the fullest consciousness, must learn to use it and must secure skilfulness in its use through conscious study. In the beginning, the best way to become acquainted with the unaccustomed functions is through very great exaggeration which must, after knowledge and technique are gained, be diminished and changed into flexible action and tension of the muscles, so that finally these are united in a machine-like harmonious whole. The apparatus must be supple, elastic in every movement and counter-movement, and obey with energy that which governs it.

Ever since Wagner made his influence felt, most singers strive to exaggerate the distinctness of the consonant, and often with them to expel the entire word in a harsh, shrill, toneless, ugly fashion; you can actually hear the end-consonants flying about in space.

Even though distinctness of articulation is necessary and desirable, the methods of the Bayreuth School were an entire failure. Their teachers, unconscious of what they were doing and teaching in good faith, committed a great wrong not only toward vocal art but toward the vocal organs of the unsuspecting singer.

Between distinct, shrill, and hard, which terms are ordinarily used synonymously, there exists a great difference.

The tongue and root of tongue are always the great evil-doers in the hard pronunciation of consonants. They compress the entire vocal apparatus of the singer and even the mere proximity of a consonant often makes impossible the pronunciation of the entire word. How unhappy artists must feel, who, when they realize such drawbacks, search for all manner of causes without being able to discover the true one. And this is because the real cause precedes the effect a long time. It is necessary to see that the tongue is put in a soft, pliable state of preparation a long time before the consonant is even thought, and is kept soft and pliable during pronunciation even though the consonant is hard.

It takes a very finely trained ear to discover the cramped and hard pronunciation of the consonants, in others or in himself. But as soon as we have discovered the origin (the tongue), our eyes are opened and we may confidently begin a new and long lasting study which is justified in taking up our entire attention.

THE ARIA OF DONNA ANNA

ANALYSIS OF THE MOVEMENT OF THE VOCAL ORGANS

Larghetto. "Über alles bleibst du theuer."
The small letters above the staff denote the forethought.

Very supple and close position of larynx on $\bar{a}$ and $\overline{oo}$. The $\bar{e}$ over the nose toward the head cavities is continually renewed, the $\overline{oo}$ is dissolved and renewed with each letter.

(The entire phrase on one breath.)

$\bar{e}$—head voice—carrying power—opens the nose.

$\bar{a}$—fixes the larynx, raises the epiglottis, secures height for the tongue, note-line, gives strength (which in this high position must only be used in a soaring manner).

$\overline{oo}$—chest voice—palatal resonance—depth—covers the tone—dissolves the form—flexibility—makes the larynx pliable.

⌒ —silent pause before double consonants and before t, k, p, upon which follows short, clear-cut pronunciation.

y—connecting medium and tension.

My Own Practice in Singing

BEFORE I close I should like to let all pass before the reader's mental eye again. I should like to tell him how I, personally, breathe, articulate, and sing.

How Do I Breathe?

The abdominal and chest pressure might still better be compared to a pair of bellows whose folds contain stagnant air just as the lower parts of the lungs contain stationary breath. Through the automatic respiration, that is, through the elastic motion of the lungs, this lowest layer of breath is then transformed into a second moving breath layer. This in turn lies above the stagnant layer. Through the automatic in- and exhalation the upper breath layer compels the cooperation of the lower one, and so produces restless, wave-like motions. We could not sing on such an unquiet surface without resorting to some remedy. Therefore we are compelled to place our organs of speech and song in such a manner, one to the other, that this unrest may be checked. So it is that a pause, arresting all movement, must be made before the word- and tone-form is placed, before the word and tone become audible. The pause serves to calm all unrest in the body, in fact, all unrest must be continually calmed after every attack, which is chiefly done by decreasing the breath. This really becomes the unceasing control of the tone.

As I have said, we continually inhale and exhale; but only during the moment of making the stagnating preparatory form and pause for speaking and singing does the inhalation and exhalation cease. It ceases as soon as it is under the control of the will power, as soon as the organs of speech and song and their muscles are definitely adjusted. Therefore it is not permissible to take a deep breath before beginning to sing, either when speaking or singing artistically, as too much breath would enter the lungs, causing a hindrance to their elastic movement. We can rid ourselves of the superfluous breath when walking or running, but never when speaking or singing artistically.

Think of a pair of bellows lying with the flat side between abdomen and chest, with the broad side front and the point in back; the upper level as the larynx, the lower one, the diaphragm, both of which must work in opposite directions so as to force the air in the bellows toward the back, from whence it streams through the larynx, and is led from here by tongue and palate to its goal.

I quickly draw in my abdomen, causing the chest, which is supported by the lower ribs, to rise; open the mouth which remains open as if I were about to speak, and out of which a little superfluous breath escapes, the moment the upward contact of the diaphragm takes place. The rest of the breath suddenly remains stationary, only taking life when tone and word begin. The nostrils also were previously inflated. That is all there is to the preparation; but there is much more which demands attention. Taking breath, then, is nothing more than a jerk exerted by the abdomen, as if, during a fright, you ejaculate an "ah!" or "oh!" whereupon all muscular functions become rigid (stiffen). To the artist, though, this rigidity is but a pause for artistic mental concentration and for muscular contraction which adjusts and unites all working forces in our body one to the other.

This art pause, the length of which is left to the judgment of the rhythmic taste of the singer, is created again and again with each new inhalation, at the beginning of every phrase, before certain consonants, before disjoined syllables and endings of syllables. It gives the artist time to test the elasticity and strength of the tension of his muscles, from top to bottom, and, though silent, it authoritatively forces the attention of the audience to his endeavors. This conscious stiffening is in reality nothing more or less than a quick mechanical adjustment of the form, which includes all that is necessary in singing.

Now we must see which course the breath takes and what we must do to prepare the best pathway as soon as the muscles of the organs are set in activity by word and tone. Just as, in singing, it is necessary to have *all* muscles coöperate so it is impossible to describe any *one* function of the vocal art without mentioning all other coöperating functions. Therefore I am obliged to repeat myself whenever I want to explain one or the other; exactly as I, the singer, must over and over again create and give life to the same placements. Right here vocal art deviates from dilettantism inasmuch as the untaught sing as they please, at one time agreeably, at another time disagreeably. The artist, however, has to create an exceedingly complicated form with all the organs of speech and tone in his body.

They are placed along an inner line from the forehead down to the diaphragm, in order to satisfy the demands of the art of song. When the jerk of inhalation takes place, the point in question is this form, which, after we have become conscious of it and mastered it, places itself instantaneously and automatically. The form consists of certain positions of nose, palate, tongue, larynx, chest, ribs, diaphragm, abdomen, and their muscles, united one to the other; it consists of muscles that tense and those of counter-tension which secure the activity and the power of endurance to the muscles and organs. We have taken a short breath; the stowed-away breath in the chest is at a stand-still. Now in order to set the machinery in action the larynx must articulate $\bar{a}$ very strongly. This tenses all muscles. It must be articulated under the drawn-back chin against the chest muscles, which thereby come in contact with the larynx and all the upper organs. Simultaneously with this larynx-$\bar{a}$ articulation toward the chest muscles, the diaphragm and abdomen make an attack from below, upward toward the chest and the larynx respectively. In the sensation it is the same $\bar{a}$ and a counter-attack, so that the breath, pushed from above downward by the larynx, and the breath, pushed from below upward by the diaphragmatic attack, meet in the chest muscles. All the tensors of all the muscles of all the vocal and respiratory organs are now joined, knit together, and constitute in the chest the "Atemstauwerk," or the chamber of breath supply, or the breath pressure.

Not until articulation begins, do the form and breath become alive. With every letter and change of tone, articulation brings about, alternately, the careful loosening and re-tensing of the muscles of the organs in the adjusted form and so keeps them alive. The articulation of the vowel $\bar{a}$ and the coöperating diaphragm force the larynx to stronger activity. Without this forward pushing of the larynx with $\bar{a}$ and $\bar{e}$ there would only be a hollow form, a bell without a clapper. If, for instance, the larynx were placed on a hollow $\overline{oo}$ without articulating $\bar{a}$, which would place the larynx between the two, there would be produced hollow, though, perhaps, large tones which many singers make use of, whose voices are simply called by the German *Ofenröhren* (stove pipes). They sound dark and hollow just as when some one toots through old lead pipes.

The larynx executes the artistic work of a clapper in this complicated and alive form. It has to strike on exact places in the adjusted form. The artistic attack which seems such a simple thing, is, in its total adjustment, extremely complicated; for it must be in perfect concord with the bell just as every muscular fibre must be in unison with the form-construction. In singing, as well as in speaking, a material, ever alive, must be dealt with.

It is much more difficult to put in action than a bell-rope, which may be grasped with the hands. It is necessary to hear with a *well-trained ear* and skilfully put together again and again that which is forever subject to change. We are dealing with living organs whose muscles, veins, arteries, and nerves are unceasingly supplied with life through the circulation of blood from the heart. All these functions are controlled by the artist's finely trained ear and by his stylistic intuition (*Stilgefühl*).

Now more of the form: As soon as we inhale with the breath-jerk, the chin falls gently downward and is pushed back close to the throat, which causes the pharynx to contract so that the back of the tongue advances high out of the throat until it reaches the back walls of the pillars of the fauces. We can soon learn to sense this by articulating the *y*-sound. The tongue then may be held on both sides with the upper molar teeth. The tip of the tongue, also drawn back, lies low in the under-jaw against the lower teeth; relaxed and yet energetic, it awaits its work. This chin-and-tongue adjustment must be retained whenever possible, or if it is altered through pronunciation it must always be renewed. It has to occur after every form-relaxation and before every breath-jerk.

The nostrils are strongly inflated. The muscles, which effect this inflation, reaching up to the cheek-bones under the eyes, are drawn up high and are placed in back of the nose broadly against the bridge of the nose. They are connected with the soft-palate peak and the pillars of the fauces, causing the sensation of a counteraction of a broad unresisting firm wall. The soft palate rises and broadens as soon as the nostrils endeavor to do the same. This produces the sensation of a broad saddle over the nose. Now this group of muscles, strongly tensed toward the back and pushed toward the front by counter-tensors, is connected with all other muscles to take up combat with them and to offer resistance.

From the strong sensation of the closely connected facial muscles, which in the beginning seem to be exceedingly pressed, and which seem to distort the face inwardly into a stiff, laughing mask, may have arisen the expression "chanter dans le masque."

All vocal art—similar to dancing and gymnastic exercise—depends on muscular tension and counter-tension; hindrances that are characteristic of body and soul. All muscles of the body, face, throat, and ears must be placed in concentrated relation. Before the actual work begins I feel as though I were drawing up toward the ears my facial and throat muscles. From there I direct all tones for tone-height.

During the singing the muscles of the abdomen which had previously been contracted are relaxed. The breath remains in the chest, held by the chest muscles of the breath pressure. The epiglottis is still closed; the nostrils are drawn broadly upward, the soft palate is pushed saddle-like forward toward them. All thought is concentrated on the articulation of the word and the tone production, but above all on the $\bar{a}$ position necessary for both. The lowered chin, the tongue, removed out of the throat and lying in the cavity of the mouth, enables the larynx, during the formation of letters and tones, to move downward, upward, backward, and forward. At all points of contact in the form, *i.e.* from above from the larynx, and from below from the diaphragm toward the chest muscles and directly on the palate where it meets with the nostril adjustment at the saddle, the attack has to take place simultaneously with the larynx-$\bar{a}$ attack. This is a single small point of meeting a centralization on a perpendicular line within the form, whose foundation is the diaphragm and chest muscles; whose towering height, the nose, palate, and tongue adjustments; whose life-giving middle is solely the larynx with its $y\bar{a}$-$y\bar{e}$-$y\overline{oo}$ articulation; whose energetic position during articulation always pushes forward and downward, fighting, together with the chest muscles, the breath that rises from the diaphragm, and so forming the supply chamber for the breath. By protecting the vocal cords from over-exertion, it teaches them to act elastically, it attracts and masters all coöperating tensors of the organs. With every change of letter or tone, which so easily endangers the form, all must be placed again and again on this perpendicular line.

In the attack the larynx finds the most energetic coöperator in the diaphragm which supports the $\bar{a}$-attack from above moving downward by an $\bar{a}$-attack from below moving upward, *i.e.* both attacks are executed simultaneously with the strongly prepared form; at the same time breath is led from the larynx with the $\bar{a}$ downward, and from the diaphragm upward. An attack is produced by the diaphragm up to the chest muscles and even up to the larynx in various degrees of strength, and according to these it may have very different effects which may be used as accent in articulation and interpretation.

To assure yourself of the coöperation of the diaphragm, which is particularly to be looked upon as the foundation of each tone, each note, each letter, each expression, and as the producer of the breath pressure, it is well to choose exercises of legato octave intervals. The moment you make the upward attack on the foundation tone with none too great an accent, you must move, with the larynx strongly articulating $\bar{a}$ down to the diaphragm (which closes the bell shape below), as if going down a contrary moving scale; while with the tongue- and palate-form $y\bar{e}$ you move quickly up the entire scale without attacking each separate tone. On the way from one interval to another, $\bar{a}y\bar{e}$, distinctly articulated, must outline the entire breath passage by a counter-movement, as if singing a sliding scale. At the same time the larynx must only hold *āyē* firmly without changing a letter and the propagating form.

In singing the regular scale in which the movement for every single tone must be heard, therefore placed, the fundamental principle of the diaphragmatic connection remains the same, with the exception that, with the fundamental tone of an upward-moving figure, the diaphragm doesn't broaden itself as much as in the case of the octave jump. But it preserves for each single tone its suitable quality and form, whereas, while practising the interval jump, the breath passage is only outlined (markiert) and only one position made—nothing should be singly placed or pronounced. The sensation of the placement for the interval jump is as that of a flat band; that of the scale closely joined pearls that are firmly bound together one to the other without having a shaking chin or larynx. The larynx always remains in close connection with the diaphragmatic, nasal, and palatal positions. Besides, these diaphragmatic effects (similar to the art of bowing, *Bogenführung*) are particularly valuable for binding one tone to another, and may be applied in sustained, classical, or also in florid songs. They must not be confounded with the often used *portamento*, which, used often, is no effect but a habit lacking in good taste.

The counter-actions of larynx and diaphragm in securing breath support may be explained as follows: The larynx with its *ā*-tension pushes the breath downward toward the chest muscles and breath pressure; the diaphragm with its counter-attack pushes the breath upward; and both meet at the point of support in the chest. (Stauwerk.) From this highly held breath restraint there escapes a very small quantity of controlled breath, passing from the Stauwerk in an indirect way through windpipe and larynx which again controls it. This minute portion of breath which is not felt, streaming upwards behind the tongue, which in turn leads it to the cavities of the head, really creates motions toward height for the tones of the scale which are produced by the downward and forward articulation of the larynx toward the point of breath support in the chest.

In doing such exercises (interval jumps) you can easily become acquainted with the counter-actions of the larynx versus diaphragm. These attacks (also called glottis stroke whenever they come in contact with the larynx ungently) may be produced in every degree of strength, according to the demands of expression. They must be ever present, never lacking; they must be made very carefully, *i.e.* very skilfully, and must be likewise applied with good taste.

The moment that articulation of a letter occurs with the adjustment vowel-*ā* of the larynx, going downward over the chest muscles to the diaphragm and abdomen, and from these again upward toward the larynx in simultaneous attack, the actual work that is the *perpetuum mobile* for tone, note, and articulation begins.

I will add that a tone without body, core, consequently an empty tone, never represents the full value of the note; and that every note is the conception of a perfect tone.

The Work of the Organs and Muscles While Singing and Articulating

The most important point after the breath-jerk, the pause, and the attack is the immediate articulation of a clear-cut *yē* with *ā*, which fully lifts the epiglottis and which connects tongue, palate, and larynx when they are *simultaneously* articulated. The *yē* changes the *ā*-placement by heightening it in back, thus enabling the *ā* to be articulated more slantingly downward in front. It also connects all letters, words, and tones one to the other, as this backward placement of the height also brings the nose and palate to a definite placement, making of them a sort of saddle from which all tones and words hang, continuing to resound. The cavity of the mouth is still more constricted. The hanging chin, sharply drawn back, is again brought nearer to the upper jaw through this compressed *yē*; the stationary breath is again decreased; the tone is not made stronger but, on the contrary, weaker.

The diaphragm is not urged on, only held quietly as a support to the tone, and by carefully diminishing the breath may be made supple. The abdomen is again drawn in so that the breath may be held quite still in the chest. Then the combined energy of *āyē* is assigned to the larynx, chest muscles, diaphragm, palate, nose, tongue, and their respective tensors and counter-tensors.

This widely ramified, extraordinarily compressed muscular exertion of the upper body concentrates itself, in my case, entirely at the ears. Here I tighten all the muscles of the head, the face, and the neck exactly as when a violin string is tuned higher and higher. Holding these muscles together as with a thread, I hang them, as it were, over the ears and from here I am able to direct them in every direction.

The form within the cavity of the mouth is constricted to the utmost by tongue and palate, making speech nearly impossible. I repeat that the *ā*-placement is changed by the *yē* and looks about like this $\bar{a}, \frac{}{\bar{a}} y^{\bar{e}}$. The larynx, raised in back by the tongue, and to which the *ā* hangs firmly, must now drive its *ā* downward in front. The sensation then is that of a perpendicular placement from the head way down to the abdomen. In this perpendicular adjustment the otherwise broadly placed *ā* can never lie excessively broad, the tone can never be pinched nor throaty, and never be flat.

The inflated nostrils, as already stated, enable the palate and nose to take a saddle-like position broadly forward, and also constrict the cavity of the mouth from above. The cavity of the mouth is now plugged up with all the organs so that hardly a particle of breath seems to get through. They thus obstruct the backward-flowing breath and prevent it from flowing out of the mouth, which, because of the extremely small space, emits only as much as is absolutely necessary. In back they are clear of the larynx, and thus enable it to operate freely when a change of letters or of pitch takes place. Likewise the tongue, freed from the larynx, though it lies apparently constricted in the cavity of the mouth, may freely use its point and back in order to lead the backward-flowing breath to the resonance cavities to which the trained ear wishes to lead it. We therefore must watch most particularly the position of the tongue in the backward part of the mouth.

Though the point of the tongue has to execute the most delicate work while articulating (but it must never stick to the upper teeth as so many lazy tongues do, stiffening the back, and putting it out of use), the singer must direct his chief attention to the back of the tongue, which must participate in the elastically energetic, but extremely difficult work of the point, and usually must react with counter-movements. To do this delicate work—I repeat—the tongue must be lifted out of the throat. This takes place when the breath-jerk is made, when the chin falls, and is pushed back, and the mouth is opened. Standing high, it frees the larynx and constricts the cavity of the mouth. The breath so hemmed in and streaming behind the tongue cannot escape directly from the mouth before it has performed its duty toward the head resonance cavities. Not until the end of a piece may it escape from the mouth on the $\bar{e}$-placement, but slowly and softly decreasing, a process for which the abdomen is entirely relaxed. But the speech- and tone-form must still be maintained for some time; all after-flowing breath must continue to resound, and be suggestive of sound to the hearer as long as the singer mentally keeps the constriction of tongue and palate. It must not be forgotten that it takes some time for a tone to resound in a large space and then to die away. At the end of every syllable, with every letter, the breath flowing in a stable narrow form under control of a steady decrease, is gently led over to the next letter. The working power of the diaphragmatic foundation, which must always be adjusted to the tone-form, must never exceed that of the laryngeal articulation, which must always remain master of the tone mechanism. The two opposite poles, larynx and diaphragm, with their counter-attacks, unfold an enormous strength, which must be kept unceasingly active toward each other by the two opponents through articulation and adjustment. Though this is the case, the powerful, but ever flexibly elastic articulation of the larynx must be the gauge for the development of power of the diaphragm. It may be made elastic in various degrees, but never let loose. The ever flexible tone which may play with the muscles, it alone is capable of expression. Soulful singing is nothing more or less than the singer's play with the muscles prompted by the heart.

The respiratory mechanism performs a breath miracle at the very moment of the short inhalation—breath-jerk—when, for example, before and during the rendition of a song, breath, barely perceptible, is taken, there is no lack of breath. Word and tone are articulated and sung in rhythm. The mouth and epiglottis are closed on the end-letters—consonants. The mouth is immediately opened again without speaking, the abdomen, which must be relaxed on each end consonant when speaking many words rapidly, is quickly drawn in, and lifts the breath to the chest where it remains many measures until the next intonation is due. The memory has placed tone- and word-form, and without renewed inhalation the singing continues. Again and again the same miracle occurs. By constricting the form so closely, breath is never needlessly lost, though it unnoticeably escapes from the mouth on the $\bar{e}$.

These small but very important preparations mentioned by me are quite sufficient, and will always be of great service in the technique of breathing; whereas the inflation of the chest and the tone made by the direct breath pressure ruin every voice, all harmonious sound, and all soulful expression.

The mask-form of the drawn-back facial muscles and of those that as counter-tension reach upward and downward constitute, then, the strong form in which the larynx, by articulating, operates like the clapper in a bell. To me it feels as strong as iron whenever I tense the muscles in strong coöperation against each other. All those muscles of the vocal organs (which are connected with these enormous tensions to perform elastic emotional work and to surround the form with a resounding, floating atmosphere), must be capable of elasticity, so much so that at the merest thought of tone coloring in articulating they expand or contract, a strong form, whose capability to expand or contract depends on the will of a skilful director. The adjustment of the organs above and below, their continual play with one another enable the directing singer to render his work in the most delightful detail. It is the connective-form which propagates itself softly and slowly from letter to letter, from tone-coloring to tone-coloring with diminishing breath, but with continual articulation of the vocal colors. These gradually bind, blend, deepen, heighten, darken, veil, lighten, strengthen, weaken, illumine, cover, let die out word and tone, strength and delicacy, without the least breath pressure; solely with the adjusted form and the skilful and flexible articulation within the form.

"Markieren"

All that I have said on short respiration with the drawn-in abdomen, the opened mouth, holding back the remaining breath with the chest muscles, etc., while making preparation to sing, is true of "markieren." "Markieren" is nothing more or less than most perfect singing, that is, the most perfect adjustment of all the organs to one another on the $\bar{a}y\bar{e}$ and $y\bar{e}\bar{a}\overline{oo}$ foundation. It differs only in that much less breath is exhaled, that change of form is avoided as much as possible, that the tensions of chest and diaphragm are held much narrower, and that articulation must proceed more gently and more in legato. Tone and word must flow easily and softly into each other and still be intelligible, without glottis, abdominal, or diaphragmatic attacks, or any other accent of strength or expression. With "markieren" the tone keeps body although diminished; it keeps its connection with the diaphragm. An endless number of phrases may thus be sung on one breath as long as there is no hindrance through unskilfulness in making the form, through breath pressure, or through articulation. To cite an example: I sang the following phrase from the Liebesduett in "Tristan und Isolde" entirely in one breath:

> "Nie wieder Erwachens, endlos
> hold bewusster Wunsch."

It is a phrase very difficult to sing in one breath after singing the taxing first and second acts. I had trained myself on the principles of "markieren" so that I could do it.

Concerning Expression

WHEN we wish to study a rôle or a song, we have first to master the intellectual content of the work. Not till we have made ourselves a clear picture of the whole should we proceed to elaborate the details, through which, however, the impression of the whole should never be allowed to suffer. The complete picture should always shine out through all. If it is too much broken into details, it becomes a thing of shreds and patches.

So petty accessories must be avoided, that the larger outline of the whole picture shall not suffer. The complete picture must ever claim the chief interest; details should not distract attention from it. In art, subordination of the parts to the whole is an art of itself. Everything must be fitted to the larger lineaments that should characterize a masterpiece.

A word is an idea; and not only the idea, but how that idea in color and connection is related to the whole, must be expressed. Therein is the fearsome magic that Wagner has exercised upon me and upon all others, that draws us to him and lets none escape its spell. That is why the elaboration of Wagner's creations seems so much worth while to the artist. Every elaboration of a work of art demands the sacrifice of some part of the artist's ego, for he must mingle the feelings set before him for portrayal with his own in his interpretation, and thus, so to speak, lay bare his very self. But since we must impersonate human beings, we may not spare ourselves, but throw ourselves into our task with the devotion of all our powers.

Before the Public

IN the wider reaches of the theatre it is needful to give an exaggeration to the expression, which in the concert hall, where the forms of society rule, must be entirely abandoned. And yet the picture must be presented by the artist to the public from the very first word, the very first note; the mood must be felt in advance. This depends partly upon the bearing of the singer and the expression of countenance he has during the prelude, whereby interest in what is coming is aroused and is directed upon the music as well as upon the poem.

The picture is complete in itself; I have only to vivify its colors during the performance. Upon the management of the body, upon the electric current which should flow between the artist and the public—a current that often streams forth at his very appearance, but often is not to be established at all—depend the glow and effectiveness of the color which we impress upon our picture.

No artist should be beguiled by this into giving forth more than artistic propriety permits, either to enhance the enthusiasm or to intensify the mood; for the electric connection cannot be forced. Often a tranquillizing feeling is very soon manifest on both sides, the effect of which is quite as great, even though less stimulating. Often, too, a calm, still understanding between singer and public exercises a fascination upon both that can only be attained through a complete devotion to the task in hand, and renunciation of any attempt to gain noisy applause.

To me it is a matter of indifference whether the public goes frantic or listens quietly and reflectively, for I give out only what I have undertaken to. If I have put my individuality, my powers, my love for the work, into a rôle or a song that is applauded by the public, I decline all thanks for it to myself personally, and consider the applause as belonging to the master whose work I am interpreting. If I have succeeded in making him intelligible to the public, the reward therefor is contained in that fact itself, and I ask for nothing more.

Of what is implied in the intelligent interpretation of a work of art, as to talent and study, the public has no conception. Only those can understand it whose lives have been devoted to the same ideals. The lasting understanding of such, or even of a part of the public, is worth more than all the storm of applause that is given to so many.

All the applause in the world cannot repay me for the sacrifices I have made for art, and no applause in the world is able to beguile me from the dissatisfaction I feel over the failure of a single tone or attempted expression.

What seems to me bad, because I demand the greatest things of myself, is, to be sure, good enough for many others. I am, however, not of their opinion. In any matter relating to art, only the best is good enough for any public. If the public is uncultivated, one must make it know the best, must educate it, must teach it to understand the best. A naïve understanding is often most strongly exhibited by the uncultivated—that is, the unspoiled—public, and often is worth more than any cultivation. The cultivated public should be willing to accept only the best; it should ruthlessly condemn the bad and the mediocre.

It is the artist's task, through offering his best and most carefully prepared achievements, to educate the public, to ennoble it; and he should carry out his mission without being influenced by bad standards of taste.

The public, on the other hand, should consider art, not as a matter of fashion, or as an opportunity to display its clothes, but should feel it as a true and profound enjoyment, and do everything to second the artist's efforts.

Arriving late at the opera or in the concert hall is a kind of bad manners which cannot be sufficiently censured. In the same way, going out before the end, at unfitting times, and the use of fans in such a way as to disturb artists and those sitting near should be avoided by cultivated people. Artists who are concentrating their whole nature upon realizing an ideal, which they wish to interpret with the most perfect expression, should not be disturbed or disquieted.

On the other hand, operatic performances, and concerts especially, should be limited in duration and in the number of pieces presented. It is better to offer the public a single symphony or a short list of songs or pianoforte pieces, which it can listen to with attention and really absorb, than to provide two or three hours of difficult music that neither the public can listen to with sufficient attention nor the artist perform with sufficient concentration.

Interpretation

LET us return to the subject of Expression, and examine a song; for example:

"Der Nussbaum," by Schumann.
The prevailing mood through it is one of quiet gayety, consequently one demanding a pleasant expression of countenance. The song picture must rustle by us like a fairy story. The picture shows us the fragrant nut tree putting forth its leaves in the spring; under it a maiden lost in revery, who finally falls asleep, happy in her thoughts. All is youth and fragrance, a charming little picture whose colors must harmonize. None of them should stand out from the frame. Only one single word rises above the rustling of the tree, and this must be brought plainly to the hearing of the listening maiden—and hence, also, of the public—the second *"next"* year. The whole song finds its point in that one word. The nut tree before the house puts forth its green leaves and sheds its fragrance; its blossoms are lovingly embraced by the soft breezes, whispering to each other two by two, and offer their heads to be kissed, nodding and bowing; the song must be sung with an equal fragrance, each musical phrase in one breath: that is, with six inaudible breathings, without ritenuto.

They whisper of a maiden who night and day is thinking, she knows not of what herself. Between "selber" and "nicht was" a slight separation of the words can be made, by breaking off the *r* in "selber" nasally; and holding the tone nasally, without taking a fresh breath, attacking the "nicht" anew. In this way an expression of uncertainty is lent to the words "nicht was."

But now all becomes quite mysterious. "They whisper, they whisper"— one must bend one's thoughts to hear it; who can understand so soft a song? But now I hear plainly, even though it be very soft—the whisper about the bridegroom and the next year, and again quite significantly, the *next* year. That is so full of promise, one can scarcely tear one's self away from the thoughts, from the word in which love is imparted, and yet that, too, comes to an end!

Now I am the maiden herself who listens, smiling in happiness, to the rustling of the tree, leaning her head against its trunk, full of longing fancies as she sinks to sleep and to dream, from which she would wish never to awaken.

"Feldeinsamkeit," by Brahms.

This song interprets the exalted mood of the soul of the man who, lying at rest in the long grass, watches the clouds float by, and whose being is made one with nature as he does so. A whole world of insects buzzes about him, the air shimmers in the bright sunlight, flowers shed their perfume; everything about him lives a murmuring life in tones that seem to enhance the peace of nature, far from the haunts of men.

As tranquil as are the clouds that pass by, as peaceful as in the mood of nature, as luxurious as are the flowers that spread their fragrance, so tranquil and calm must be the breathing of the singer, which draws the long phrases of the song over the chords of the accompaniment, and brings before us in words and tones the picture of the warm peace of summer in nature, and the radiant being of a man dissolved within it.

I mark the breathing places with V. "Ich liege still im hohen grünen Grass V und sende lange meinen Blick V nach oben V [and again comfortably, calmly] nach oben.

"Von Grillen rings umschwärmt V ohn' Unterlass V von Himmelsbläue wundersam umwoben V von Himmelsbläue V *wundersam umwoben.*"

Each tone, each letter, is connected closely with the preceding and following; the expression of the eyes and of the soul should be appropriate to that of the glorified peace of nature and of the soul's happiness. The last phrase should soar tenderly, saturated with a warm and soulful coloring.

"Die schönen weissen Wolken zieh'n dahin V durch's *tiefe* Blau V, [I gaze at it for a moment] wie schöne, stille Träume V [losing one's self] wie schöne, stille Träume. V [A feeling of dissolution takes away every thought of living and being.] Mir ist V als ob V ich längst V gestorben bin! [The whole being is dissolved in the other; the end comes with outstretched wings soaring above the earth.] Und ziehe selig mit V durch ew'ge Räume V und ziehe selig mit V durch ew'ge Räume." [Dissolution of the soul in the universe must sound forth from the singer's tone.]

"The Erlking," by Schubert.

For him who is familiar with our native legends and tales, the willows and alders in the fields and by the brooks are peopled with hidden beings, fairies, and witches. They stretch out ghostly arms, as their veils wave over their loose hair, they bow, cower, raise themselves, become as big as giants or as little as dwarfs. They seem to lie in wait for the weak, to fill them with fright.

The father, however, who rides with his child through the night and the wind, is a man, no ghost; and his faithful steed, that carries both, no phantom. The picture is presented to us vividly; we can follow the group for long. The feeling is of haste, but not of ghostliness. The prelude should consequently sound simply fast, but not overdrawn. The first phrases of the singer should be connected with it as a plain narrative.

Suddenly the child hugs the father more closely and buries his face in terror in his bosom. Lovingly the father bends over him; *quietly* he asks him the cause of his fear.

Frightened, the child looks to one side, and asks, in disconnected phrases, whether his father does not see the Erlking, the Erlking with his crown and train. They had just ridden by a clump of willows. Still quietly, the father explains *smilingly* to his son that what he saw was a bank of fog hanging over the meadow.

But in the boy's brain the Erlking has already raised his enticing whisper.[1] The still, small voice, as though coming from another world, promises the child golden raiment, flowers, and games.

Fearfully he asks his father if he does not hear the Erlking's whispered promises.

"It is only the dry leaves rustling in the wind." The father quiets him, and his voice is full of firm and loving reassurance, but he feels that his child is sick.

For but a few seconds all is still; then the voice comes back again. In a low whisper sounds and words are distinguished. The Erlking invites the boy to play with his daughters, who shall dance with him and rock him and sing to him.

In the heat of fever the boy implores his father to look for the Erlking's daughters. The father sees only an old gray willow; but his voice is no longer calm. Anxiety for his sick child makes his manly tones break; the

---

[1] The voice of the Erlking is a continuous, soft, uninterrupted stream of tone, upon which the whispered words are hung. The Erlking excites the thoughts of the fever-sick boy. The three enticements must be sung very rapidly, without any interruption of the breath. The first I sing as far as possible in one breath (if I am not hampered by the accompanist), or at most in two; the second in two, the third in three; and here for the first time the words "reizt" and "brauch ich Gewalt" emerge from the whispered pianissimo.

comforting words contain already a longing for the journey's end—
quickly, quickly, must he reach it.

The Erlking has now completely filled the feverish fancy of the child.
With ruthless power he possesses himself of the boy—all opposition is
vain—the silver cord is loosened. Once more he cries out in fear to his
father, then his eyes are closed. The man, beside himself, strains every
nerve—his own and his horse's; his haste is like a wild flight. The
journey's end is reached; breathless they stop—but the race was in vain.

A cold shudder runs through even the narrator; his whole being is
strained and tense, he must force his mouth to utter the last words.

"Der Spielmann," by Schumann.

If the critics were to study as eagerly as the finished artist, there would
be enough material on hand for stimulating discussions from which the
public at large would profit.

Thus lying before me is a letter on music wherein one of my last
concerts, but more especially Schumann's "Spielmann," is the theme of
discussion. Would it not be interesting to the public to learn how such
songs find interpretation in the artist?

This song had long claimed my attention. The text is constructed on
one idea in which the fate of three human beings is decided in cruel
shortness of time. This appealed to me—an interesting picture and a well-
adapted composition.

A small rural wedding with music and dance; the pale bride, the
"Spielmann" who is not the bridegroom but who plays for the dance,
pressing the fiddle so strongly against his heart that it breaks in a thousand
pieces—a compassionate spectator to whom it is painful to see so young a
heart, which craves for happiness, perish. The "Spielmann's" sudden
outburst of insanity puts an end to his meditation. A poor "Musikant"
lowers his frightened glance and prays to God to save him from such a
terrible end.

The whole song is over in a flash. One only begins to comprehend it at
the outburst of insanity, and before one has fully realized all, the poor
"Musikant" has finished his prayer and then, very softly, as from a great
distance, a faint strain of the dance-melody reaches our ear.

It is seen how everything concentrates itself on the insane outburst; and
yet to this phrase, like all others composed on three notes of the middle
range, accents of expression cannot be given. But I attempt it. The song is
mine. I possess it absolutely and in my inmost soul know how it ought to
sound. I must cry it out from the depth of my soul, with all pain and
grief, cry it, declaiming it.

No, not yet. I again strive to follow the composer. I sing the passage a hundred times this way and that and still another way. My listeners, that is my family or an intimate friend, think it excellent. I am indignant. What do they understand! I feel that the effect must be quite different. I can get it vocally and as in a picture I can characterize the insanity with widely dilated, terrified eyes and gnashing teeth, vivid enough to affect a few people who stand near, but how can it be effective in a hall that seats 2000 people? Yes, even in a spacious room it would merely be a thought and not action, and action it must nearly be—nearly, not quite.

Despite all reverence for the composer, or rather because I want to do him justice, I must cry it out with all my heart from my inmost self and now—now I feel released. This is what I needed. There remains only to establish the limit, the just measure of beauty, and the end is attained, and then I have made it mine. The given music now facilitates matters, and I follow the composer's restrictions, not too high, not too low, only the exact tone appropriate to a tormented soul in a song of modest limits. Now devoting a couple of weeks to diligent study, I am able to do justice to Schumann's composition.

No, I am no friend of extremes. Everything has its limits, and art especially must ever be mindful of it. Neither in grief nor in happiness, in gentleness nor in brutality, may we indulge in exaggeration. We must never go beyond the line of beauty. In only a few cases may genius be allowed to overstep the bounds, but this exaggeration is only produced through sublimity of expression, not through brutality.

I am reminded of the answer given me by a celebrated Shakespearean actress upon being asked if she had acted the part of *Juliet*: "I'll not act Juliet until I am a grandmother!" The response is significant of the respect which certain rôles inspire in great artists. They labor over them a lifetime, never thinking them fit for presentation.

In a small way I too can furnish an example of these scruples. As a young girl I sang with great pleasure Schumann's "Frauenliebe und Leben." Later I let it alone. I realized more and more how deep, how great, certain ones are—such a world of feeling—is it really possible to sing them? It seemed to me that I was too weak for the task, and yet how gladly I would sing them! Alas! There is no prospect of my ever becoming a grandmother.

I herewith draw attention to six magnificent concert arias by Mozart, three dramatic and three coloratura. To the latter were added two more taken from the C minor Mass. They have been edited by Peters and I gave them a new German text and the following preface:

PREFACE

So that capable artists may become better acquainted with some of
Mozart's concert arias, I have supplied them, especially the recitatives,
with improved German text which does more justice to the original text,
as well as to the accents of Mozart's great art, and the dramatic
interpretative ability of the singer. At the present time the original Italian
text does not suffice; we wish to sing in our mother tongue which possesses
enough strength and poesy to express everything that art demands. I have
bestowed much love on this work. May it bring fame and honor to the
artist, may it give him that contentment found in the rendition of noble
works of art.

Declaim and sing the recitatives on a large scale, broadly, in the fullest
agreement with modern interpretation, vivifying a theatrical scene; for this
the aria of *Andromeda* is especially suitable. Mozart was no pedant, no
school teacher; he made concessions to his artists, and left to the singer
what was his, as all great musicians of their times did. Let us hold to that.

Do not sing Mozart in metronome rhythm. With his music you may
well think of the best, repressed Italian music. Never divest word and note
of their soulful accents of emotions so as to condemn them to a monotony
which some would designate as classical; for we live through the fate of
those persons whom we vocally or scenically represent. Hans von Bülow
once said in my presence, "Music is rhythm," and Gustav Mahler at
another time remarked, "One measure is never like another." Both were
quite right. A short or long word on notes of the same value may never be
treated alike, either by singer or conductor.

To a fixed rhythm—despite the liberty that may be taken in the
interpretation of recitatives—I count most particularly the pauses in which
the singer has just concluded a phrase and is about to begin another which
belongs to it, or a new one. To control herewith the mental authority of
artistic expectancy, and likewise also the resuming of the concentration of
all organs of speech and tensed breath closely allied to it, to transmit this
to rhythm and expression in word and tone, belongs to the most difficult,
the most unknown, and the never taught problem of the art of song. All
of the technique of breathing depends on it. It could be learned quickly
and well by acquiring certain little habits. I say "could be learned," but it
is not seriously paid attention to by the singer, to say nothing of the
student, because he never seems to become conscious of the great
advantage gained by taking pains to think of it incessantly.

Even if not indicated, the rhythm must sometimes be hastened a little
or sometimes not noticeably broadened. Naturally it is necessary to have
a fine stylistic intuition to make such fine shading, to have authority that

comes from knowledge and which the artist must acquire. Those who cannot master this should seek advice from the better informed; that is no disgrace. It is the same with the appoggiatura on two end notes of the sound; it isn't always necessary to make them, but at the same time they cannot be entirely done away with, especially not in the recitatives. Without them the music, as well as the declamation, sounds dead; all life is withdrawn from the expression of the word.

Also nothing should prevent you from cutting short the repetitions in the *allegro tempi*, unimportant for the word; a question, however, to be settled between artist and conductor. Mozart's music would of course pass muster without this abridgement; on the other hand, its value would not be lessened by making the cuts, since these were very often concessions made to the singers of those days, or they were the customary musical form of the day.

In the coloratura arias of the second book, I repeat, especial modifications in tempo may be made so that the beautiful embellishments do not resemble solfeggios or pedantry. The arias must be sung with much "élan," tempo hastened here, slackened there, just as it suits the skill and power of expression of a good artist, and her physical condition. At any rate, intensified coloraturas are sung best on a stronger tensed breath; great heights and quiet figures on a decreasing breath. Here as everywhere the conductor must further the cause (he should never look at the notes, but keep his attention fixed on the singer's mouth). He must never endanger the artistically beautiful structure by his own stubbornness. I do not mean to say, however, that every singer should have full power. The Kapellmeister has to give the accompaniment a consistent, life-giving style, and combine rhythm with good taste—to make of it a model.

If we transfer the so-called Italian style to German feeling and seriousness without taking away the warmth of expression, if we cleanse it of exaggerations, which, by the way, the noble Italian singer is less guilty of than the German, we are well justifed in interpreting Mozart, Beethoven, and others in the good Italian style. In this way I took great pleasure in singing Wagner's music, for example, "Tristan und Isolde" in a beautiful legato in the fine Italian style; for after all there is only one perfect art of song.

LILLI LEHMANN.

BERLIN, December, 1920.

Indispositions

IN the supposition of being called from earth to-day or to-morrow I would not like the following article to remain unwritten, for I believe that singer as well as doctor may gain therefrom.

So often I have wished to explain at length the many difficult situations in which the singer through change of temperature or climate, colds, nervous influences of various kinds, or through the spite of inanimate objects may so often be placed, that I will set forth just a few interesting and instructive examples which have happened to me.

To begin, a little Richard Wagner anecdote: On the 12th of May, 1872, Richard Wagner directed a concert in Vienna in which the horn virtuoso, Richard Levy, broke on a note, making a squeaking sound ("gigsen"), which caused the audience to laugh. After the concert when we were all gathered in the artists' room, Wagner declared it a crime to ridicule a hornist on account of "gigsen." It were well to understand what it really meant to obtain an ideal tone from base metal, and how a tiny drop of saliva could cause the greatest virtuoso to founder.

I have already mentioned how the still youthful Max Staegemann and the not much older Pauline Lucca complained about continual catarrh and from suffering from phlegm which made it impossible for them to keep up their professions as singers. I naturally should never have given my catarrh that power, but, like all singers, I had, and still have, to suffer from it. Also Jean de Reszke, that magnificent artist, told me, when speaking of it: "Chère Mme. Lehmann j'ai craché toute ma vie." And so it happens to many of us, often to very young singers, if they happen to be particularly sensitive to colds.

How often it happens that one comes to a concert in splendid trim only to be met by a cool wind at the very first entrance. The difference in temperature between artists' room and hall very often with the first inhalation causes a clearing of the throat, loosening small particles of phlegm which in the constantly outflowing breath move to and fro completely spoiling one's pleasure in the concert, as they absorb the singer's entire attention in the in- and exhalations. If they are happily situated they are sometimes quite loosened with the first number, very often, however, not for half, or even all the evening, when they, ad libitum, change places on the in- and exhalations. Sometimes even a single little thread lying across the vocal cords may spoil everything, and not seldom friend Landecker hears at the close of a concert, "Now at last I am rid of the little thread which has annoyed me the whole evening." One can't clear or cough it away, neither during the concert, nor during the singing.

I, personally, as one old in experience, am always very careful in placing my tongue in such a manner in the open mouth that pharynx and larynx are never exposed to cold air without a covering. Sometimes even this is not enough protection, and in spite of most careful precaution and with all my experience I am not always successful in completely or nearly evading or eliminating the little threads which I touch as lightly as possible with my breath. He who has a task to perform must go through with it, must solve it as best he can, must never give up the game. The listener has only the idea of the singer or actor's "indisposition," but that this is caused by a little thread of phlegm momentarily set in motion, he naturally has not the slightest notion. Fortunately the opposite sometimes happens—that one isn't in especially good condition at home, and the evening passes splendidly. Such agreeable disappointments belong to the happiest events of an artist's life.

This is a side issue. More difficult problems make their appearance which we artists can reach only through knowledge, and which are far more interesting than small occasional phlegm-thread-strayings, often of only a minute's duration.

Now I must mention a strange indisposition which carries in it the explanation of a far worse one of at least twenty years before.

Following a long and stubborn case of "grippe" with violent cough came a quarter of a year of complete restoration to health and much singing. Every morning as soon as I got up and dressed, I sang chromatic and other scales to give the larynx through gymnastic exercise the necessary elasticity—also a means of preservation. I often felt at that time that my larynx responded less readily than before to the usual motions, and jokingly said to the others, "I have a billiard ball in my throat." None of my exercises brought me any improvement of motion-possibilities in coloraturas, which I could perform quite well but without the usual tone-strength. This, of course, was felt only by me, and was noticed by no one else. I calculated then that there must be something in my larynx offering resistance, described the spot and the sensation to our dear Sanitätsrat Wernicke very accurately, and begged him to examine my throat most carefully. Following my exact description he soon unravelled the mystery. Between true and false, or upper and lower vocal cords a little lump of phlegm had fastened itself, causing the insufficient motion of the larynx. Otherwise everything was found in perfect condition. To loosen it by coughing or clearing the throat was impossible at this point, so nothing remained but to gargle often and very slowly with Emser water or camomile tea, and to stop up the nose with a soothing balsam, that is, lanolin and menthol which cause a dissolution, and stimulate the mucous membranes to activity. A considerable time passed before the dissolution was complete, and quite a long time before everything in the runs and scales worked to my satisfaction. In the meantime I went to Salzburg to open the Mozart-course and here in the course of the dissolution long afterwards a periodic hoarseness, which affected even my speech, set in for hours at a time, and then disappeared as suddenly as it had come. Highly interesting were other effects of this dissolution in the form of the strangest phenomena. One morning, on the road to complete vocal clearness, while I was singing big exercises, I went in slow scale to the high *b*, held it long, and allowed it in diminishing breath to die out. Suddenly the tone leapt—I had robbed it of support—to the *b* on the fifth ledger line, where I was able to hold it, and, without spoiling the form, to repeatedly attack it. I tried the experiment before my pupils, and, although they were accustomed to hear me sing daily the high *e*, *f*, *f* sharp and *g*, they marvelled at this wonder, which simply arose from the fact that a small particle of phlegm, having become loosened, spread itself across the vocal cords, thereby simply separating the upper from the under tone. The original cause was the "grippe" cough in which with main force I had drawn the secretion toward the larynx where it remained fastened. Soon, however, I was entirely freed from this condition.

But now I shall revert to the much more difficult case reaching far back to the time in America when I was forced to discontinue singing for a period of four weeks during the season.

We had just completed under Maurice Grau one of the most unforget-able of Tristan performances with Jean and Eduard de Reszke. The curtain had fallen, the dead were about to arise. The motion of the many costumes, the falling of the curtain, and the continual shower of impregnating material had stirred up much dust, and very likely in talking with my colleagues I had gotten some of it in my windpipe, for suddenly a terrible coughing spell developed whose irritation tantalized me until it and I were completely exhausted. Arrived at the hotel, we were forced to wait around in draughty halls for almost an hour, as fire had broken out, and we were not able to get to our apartments until it was put out. Strange to say the next day I was quite well. Not until evening did a hoarseness develop. In a short time I could hardly speak, and had the feeling of a badly swollen larynx. The next night I was compelled to call off the "Götterdämmerung." And now a very uncomfortable time began for me. The hoarseness did not budge from the spot. After a few days Grau sent me Dr. Curtis, a very famous American doctor, and a very pleasant gentleman, with the object of making an examination. He was to tell him when I would be available again. Dr. Curtis said that my throat was in good condition, that he couldn't find anything the matter, and that I could sing in three or four days. I was furious. I could hardly speak, hadn't a tone in my throat, and nothing the matter? I should even sing in a couple of days! I believe I rebuked good Dr. Curtis in no gentle manner. He then begged me to come to his office next day where he discovered a little inflammation on one vocal cord (perhaps just to quiet me), and wished to use electricity outwardly. As this seemed to have absolutely no effect on my condition, I put an end to the matter by singing exercises on my own responsibility. To this Dr. Curtis entirely acquiesced. With a few free tones in the middle range I made connection from one tone to another with $\bar{a}$, $\bar{a}\bar{e}$, $\bar{a}y\bar{e}$, and so continually increased the intervals. It went very slowly, but after a time the old accustomed life began to return to the muscles of my larynx (I can't recall if excretions took place at that time). After four weeks, I was at last able to appear as *Berta* in the "Prophet."

Here also various phenomena made their appearance, since every few hours I was differently disposed. Now I had gigantic height and little depth, and immediately following a middle voice of unheard-of strength, while another part of the voice was considerably weakened. Often I was compelled during my singing to invent other words with light or dark vowels so that I could maintain a well-sounding tone here and there. Unswerving exercises for speech and song soon regulated these appearances. With each rôle I felt an improvement and the horrible condition disappearing. After a short time the whole Metropolitan Opera Company travelled to London for the season where in about five weeks I sang sixteen large rôles. At the first "Norma" rehearsal something happened which occurred again twenty years later. In a very high part which I tried entirely pianissimo my voice broke and went an octave higher, the fourth ledger line above the staff, from which place I sang the whole rôle to the end to the speechless astonishment of Kapellmeister Mancinelli and the orchestra, to whom I laughingly explained the phenomenon which they had never met or heard of.

When at the present day I compare these two indispositions, I am forced involuntarily to see their similarity. To-day I am not at all astonished that Dr. Curtis did not find anything the matter with my throat at that time, since the cause—the coughed-in dust and saliva which had balled itself between the pair of vocal cords—was tightly wedged in a surely not to be recognized spot, and which so many years later charmed into life the pretty playful four-lined octave phenomenon. But this may also be accomplished in quite a natural way, by not making the contact with the chest muscles and certain tongue and palate adjustments.

A further uncanny indisposition befell me at one time when, after an engagement on the Rhine in 1909, I hurriedly travelled to Vienna to begin there a longer engagement with Verdi's "Requiem" given under the leadership of Weingartner for the benefit of the Philharmonic widows and orphans. How I looked forward to singing this magnificent and beloved composition which I had sung under the personal leadership of Verdi in Cologne, and later many times in Berlin. Immediately upon my arrival at the piano-rehearsal, my breath caused me great anxiety. It was impossible for me to exhale, that is, I didn't seem to be able to get rid of my breath. This feeling of inflated lungs which never relaxed was horrible! Since I hardly draw breath, always sing with diminished breath which streams out in flowing currents, I never feel the necessity of inflating my lungs. The next day at the orchestra-rehearsal the case was aggravated. I felt as if my lungs must burst; and on the concert evening it became so serious that I was not able to sing the second last, most difficult number, "Requiem Æternam," which demands a continuous held-back breath. I was forced to omit it. Of the cause of this trouble I had no idea, but laid it to the long journey; and after several days the strange feeling was gone. I was able to perform my engagement as guest. Arrived at home I received the explanation of this terrible attack through Madam Gadsky, who called on me immediately after her return from America. "Oh, that is a well-known condition in America, which often occurs after travelling great distances. Everywhere you find in readiness hydrogen peroxide apparatus which removes the trouble in a half hour." The cause in Vienna was also the rapid change of climate. In America in all my long journeys it had never happened to me. I wish never again to be placed in such a terrible condition.

It was in New York in the winter of 1902, that I arrived in brilliant condition at a matinee recital at Carnegie Hall. During the first three numbers a very strange feeling came over nose, mouth, and lips, from which I could not free myself. Finally my lips stuck so fast to my teeth that I could hardly separate them. What could that possibly be! I reflected. I certainly had been perfectly healthy when I came to the concert. My head began to swim, and the heat on the stage became unbearable. Though not noticeable to others, I was in a desperate frame of mind. Arrived at home I had but the one thought. I was going to be ill. I couldn't quench my thirst; therefore, a probable case of fever or influenza. But I didn't get sick, and the next day it was all gone. On close examination I found out that hot-air pipes in the front wall of the stage on which I stood, threw heat waves of dry air directly in my face, which, in inhalation, had completely dried out the mucous membrane. Naturally I had no idea of the absurdity of such an arrangement which pumped hot air directly into a singer's face, thereby drying out his throat to the point of strangulation.

That as a seventeen-year-old beginner in Prague I sang, acted, and exercised in a rôle in the pretty "Weiber von Georgien," after having been bent double with pain all day from an attack of lumbago—mamma carrying me to the carriage—was a very painful, but not especially artistic feat . . . More agreeable is an experience in Berlin, where, poisoned by a lobster mayonnaise, I was unable for fourteen days, through severe pain, either to open my mouth or bring my teeth together, and yet I had to sing great rôles at the same time. I will barely mention the many sore throats with which we Lehmanns sang, and of which we never took notice.

But to come back to the object. In Vienna, while singing the *Desdemona* in Verdi's "Othello," my sister had stuck a large nail in her foot, and was compelled to sing and act the entire final scene before she could gain relief. This and other jokes and spites of objects, of course play no important part by the side of serious physical or soul-stirring indispositions. Surely all artists have like experiences; perhaps they are not always of so light a nature, or end so happily. Not seldom they leave traces of deep pain in recollection and have even threatened, poisoned, if not prematurely ended, the life of many an artist. These, naturally, must be reckoned as representing the more unfortunate of cases.

Nevertheless an artist is often able through his very profession to nip many a disease in the bud, to throw it entirely off. The excitement of appearing before an audience with a great task, the necessity of concentrating his bodily strength to the utmost, even through increased perspiration, these things bring physical advantages hardly believable which only he learns to know who possesses courage and energy enough to put implicit faith in himself and in all that the nerves are capable of doing.

In Conclusion

THE class of voice is dependent upon the inborn characteristics of the vocal organs. But the development of the voice and all else that appertains to the art of song can, providing talent is not lacking, be learned through industry and energy.

If every singer cannot become a *famous* artist, every singer is at least in duty bound to have learned something worth while, and to do his best according to his powers, as soon as he has to appear before any public. As an artist, he should not afford this public merely a cheap amusement, but should acquaint it with the most perfect embodiments of that art whose sole task properly is to ennoble the taste of mankind, and to bestow happiness; to raise it above the miseries of this workaday world, withdraw it from those miseries, to idealize even the hateful things in human nature which it may have to represent, without departing from truth.

But what is the attitude of artists toward these tasks?

NOTE

A Good Remedy for Catarrh and Hoarseness

Pour boiling hot water into a saucer, and let a large sponge suck it all up. Then squeeze it firmly out again. Hold the sponge to the nose and mouth, and breathe alternately through the nose and mouth, in and out.

I sing my exercises, the great scale, passages, etc., and all the vowels into it, and so force the hot steam to act upon the lungs, bronchial tubes, and especially on the mucous membranes, while I am breathing in and out through the sponge. After this has been kept up for ten or fifteen minutes, wash the face in cold water. This can be repeated four to six times a day. The sponge should be full of water, but must be quite squeezed out. This has helped me greatly, and I can recommend it highly. It can do no injury because it is natural. But after breathing in the hot steam, do not go out immediately into the cold air.

A CATALOG OF SELECTED
DOVER BOOKS
IN ALL FIELDS OF INTEREST

A CATALOG OF SELECTED DOVER
BOOKS IN ALL FIELDS OF INTEREST

CONCERNING THE SPIRITUAL IN ART, Wassily Kandinsky. Pioneering work by father of abstract art. Thoughts on color theory, nature of art. Analysis of earlier masters. 12 illustrations. 80pp. of text. 5⅜ x 8½.   23411-8

ANIMALS: 1,419 Copyright-Free Illustrations of Mammals, Birds, Fish, Insects, etc., Jim Harter (ed.). Clear wood engravings present, in extremely lifelike poses, over 1,000 species of animals. One of the most extensive pictorial sourcebooks of its kind. Captions. Index. 284pp. 9 x 12.   23766-4

CELTIC ART: The Methods of Construction, George Bain. Simple geometric techniques for making Celtic interlacements, spirals, Kells-type initials, animals, humans, etc. Over 500 illustrations. 160pp. 9 x 12. (Available in U.S. only.)   22923-8

AN ATLAS OF ANATOMY FOR ARTISTS, Fritz Schider. Most thorough reference work on art anatomy in the world. Hundreds of illustrations, including selections from works by Vesalius, Leonardo, Goya, Ingres, Michelangelo, others. 593 illustrations. 192pp. 7⅛ x 10¼.   20241-0

CELTIC HAND STROKE-BY-STROKE (Irish Half-Uncial from "The Book of Kells"): An Arthur Baker Calligraphy Manual, Arthur Baker. Complete guide to creating each letter of the alphabet in distinctive Celtic manner. Covers hand position, strokes, pens, inks, paper, more. Illustrated. 48pp. 8¼ x 11.   24336-2

EASY ORIGAMI, John Montroll. Charming collection of 32 projects (hat, cup, pelican, piano, swan, many more) specially designed for the novice origami hobbyist. Clearly illustrated easy-to-follow instructions insure that even beginning papercrafters will achieve successful results. 48pp. 8¼ x 11.   27298-2

THE COMPLETE BOOK OF BIRDHOUSE CONSTRUCTION FOR WOODWORKERS, Scott D. Campbell. Detailed instructions, illustrations, tables. Also data on bird habitat and instinct patterns. Bibliography. 3 tables. 63 illustrations in 15 figures. 48pp. 5¼ x 8½.   24407-5

BLOOMINGDALE'S ILLUSTRATED 1886 CATALOG: Fashions, Dry Goods and Housewares, Bloomingdale Brothers. Famed merchants' extremely rare catalog depicting about 1,700 products: clothing, housewares, firearms, dry goods, jewelry, more. Invaluable for dating, identifying vintage items. Also, copyright-free graphics for artists, designers. Co-published with Henry Ford Museum & Greenfield Village. 160pp. 8¼ x 11.   25780-0

HISTORIC COSTUME IN PICTURES, Braun & Schneider. Over 1,450 costumed figures in clearly detailed engravings–from dawn of civilization to end of 19th century. Captions. Many folk costumes. 256pp. 8⅜ x 11¾.   23150-X

STICKLEY CRAFTSMAN FURNITURE CATALOGS, Gustav Stickley and L. & J. G. Stickley. Beautiful, functional furniture in two authentic catalogs from 1910. 594 illustrations, including 277 photos, show settles, rockers, armchairs, reclining chairs, bookcases, desks, tables. 183pp. 6½ x 9¼. 23838-5

AMERICAN LOCOMOTIVES IN HISTORIC PHOTOGRAPHS: 1858 to 1949, Ron Ziel (ed.). A rare collection of 126 meticulously detailed official photographs, called "builder portraits," of American locomotives that majestically chronicle the rise of steam locomotive power in America. Introduction. Detailed captions. xi+ 129pp. 9 x 12. 27393-8

AMERICA'S LIGHTHOUSES: An Illustrated History, Francis Ross Holland, Jr. Delightfully written, profusely illustrated fact-filled survey of over 200 American lighthouses since 1716. History, anecdotes, technological advances, more. 240pp. 8 x 10¾. 25576-X

TOWARDS A NEW ARCHITECTURE, Le Corbusier. Pioneering manifesto by founder of "International School." Technical and aesthetic theories, views of industry, economics, relation of form to function, "mass-production split" and much more. Profusely illustrated. 320pp. 6⅛ x 9¼. (Available in U.S. only.) 25023-7

HOW THE OTHER HALF LIVES, Jacob Riis. Famous journalistic record, exposing poverty and degradation of New York slums around 1900, by major social reformer. 100 striking and influential photographs. 233pp. 10 x 7⅞. 22012-5

FRUIT KEY AND TWIG KEY TO TREES AND SHRUBS, William M. Harlow. One of the handiest and most widely used identification aids. Fruit key covers 120 deciduous and evergreen species; twig key 160 deciduous species. Easily used. Over 300 photographs. 126pp. 5⅜ x 8½. 20511-8

COMMON BIRD SONGS, Dr. Donald J. Borror. Songs of 60 most common U.S. birds: robins, sparrows, cardinals, bluejays, finches, more—arranged in order of increasing complexity. Up to 9 variations of songs of each species.
Cassette and manual 99911-4

ORCHIDS AS HOUSE PLANTS, Rebecca Tyson Northen. Grow cattleyas and many other kinds of orchids—in a window, in a case, or under artificial light. 63 illustrations. 148pp. 5⅜ x 8½. 23261-1

MONSTER MAZES, Dave Phillips. Masterful mazes at four levels of difficulty. Avoid deadly perils and evil creatures to find magical treasures. Solutions for all 32 exciting illustrated puzzles. 48pp. 8¼ x 11. 26005-4

MOZART'S DON GIOVANNI (DOVER OPERA LIBRETTO SERIES), Wolfgang Amadeus Mozart. Introduced and translated by Ellen H. Bleiler. Standard Italian libretto, with complete English translation. Convenient and thoroughly portable—an ideal companion for reading along with a recording or the performance itself. Introduction. List of characters. Plot summary. 121pp. 5¼ x 8½. 24944-1

TECHNICAL MANUAL AND DICTIONARY OF CLASSICAL BALLET, Gail Grant. Defines, explains, comments on steps, movements, poses and concepts. 15-page pictorial section. Basic book for student, viewer. 127pp. 5⅜ x 8½. 21843-0

THE CLARINET AND CLARINET PLAYING, David Pino. Lively, comprehensive work features suggestions about technique, musicianship, and musical interpretation, as well as guidelines for teaching, making your own reeds, and preparing for public performance. Includes an intriguing look at clarinet history. "A godsend," The Clarinet, Journal of the International Clarinet Society. Appendixes. 7 illus. 320pp. 5⅜ x 8½.   40270-3

HOLLYWOOD GLAMOR PORTRAITS, John Kobal (ed.). 145 photos from 1926-49. Harlow, Gable, Bogart, Bacall; 94 stars in all. Full background on photographers, technical aspects. 160pp. 8⅜ x 11¼.   23352-9

THE ANNOTATED CASEY AT THE BAT: A Collection of Ballads about the Mighty Casey/Third, Revised Edition, Martin Gardner (ed.). Amusing sequels and parodies of one of America's best-loved poems: Casey's Revenge, Why Casey Whiffed, Casey's Sister at the Bat, others. 256pp. 5⅜ x 8½.   28598-7

THE RAVEN AND OTHER FAVORITE POEMS, Edgar Allan Poe. Over 40 of the author's most memorable poems: "The Bells," "Ulalume," "Israfel," "To Helen," "The Conqueror Worm," "Eldorado," "Annabel Lee," many more. Alphabetic lists of titles and first lines. 64pp. 5³⁄₁₆ x 8¼.   26685-0

PERSONAL MEMOIRS OF U. S. GRANT, Ulysses Simpson Grant. Intelligent, deeply moving firsthand account of Civil War campaigns, considered by many the finest military memoirs ever written. Includes letters, historic photographs, maps and more. 528pp. 6⅛ x 9¼.   28587-1

ANCIENT EGYPTIAN MATERIALS AND INDUSTRIES, A. Lucas and J. Harris. Fascinating, comprehensive, thoroughly documented text describes this ancient civilization's vast resources and the processes that incorporated them in daily life, including the use of animal products, building materials, cosmetics, perfumes and incense, fibers, glazed ware, glass and its manufacture, materials used in the mummification process, and much more. 544pp. 6¹⁄₈ x 9¹⁄₄. (Available in U.S. only.)   40446-3

RUSSIAN STORIES/RUSSKIE RASSKAZY: A Dual-Language Book, edited by Gleb Struve. Twelve tales by such masters as Chekhov, Tolstoy, Dostoevsky, Pushkin, others. Excellent word-for-word English translations on facing pages, plus teaching and study aids, Russian/English vocabulary, biographical/critical introductions, more. 416pp. 5⅜ x 8½.   26244-8

PHILADELPHIA THEN AND NOW: 60 Sites Photographed in the Past and Present, Kenneth Finkel and Susan Oyama. Rare photographs of City Hall, Logan Square, Independence Hall, Betsy Ross House, other landmarks juxtaposed with contemporary views. Captures changing face of historic city. Introduction. Captions. 128pp. 8¼ x 11.   25790-8

AIA ARCHITECTURAL GUIDE TO NASSAU AND SUFFOLK COUNTIES, LONG ISLAND, The American Institute of Architects, Long Island Chapter, and the Society for the Preservation of Long Island Antiquities. Comprehensive, well-researched and generously illustrated volume brings to life over three centuries of Long Island's great architectural heritage. More than 240 photographs with authoritative, extensively detailed captions. 176pp. 8¼ x 11.   26946-9

NORTH AMERICAN INDIAN LIFE: Customs and Traditions of 23 Tribes, Elsie Clews Parsons (ed.). 27 fictionalized essays by noted anthropologists examine religion, customs, government, additional facets of life among the Winnebago, Crow, Zuni, Eskimo, other tribes. 480pp. 6⅛ x 9¼.   27377-6

FRANK LLOYD WRIGHT'S DANA HOUSE, Donald Hoffmann. Pictorial essay of residential masterpiece with over 160 interior and exterior photos, plans, elevations, sketches and studies. 128pp. 9¼ x 10¾. 29120-0

THE MALE AND FEMALE FIGURE IN MOTION: 60 Classic Photographic Sequences, Eadweard Muybridge. 60 true-action photographs of men and women walking, running, climbing, bending, turning, etc., reproduced from rare 19th-century masterpiece. vi + 121pp. 9 x 12. 24745-7

1001 QUESTIONS ANSWERED ABOUT THE SEASHORE, N. J. Berrill and Jacquelyn Berrill. Queries answered about dolphins, sea snails, sponges, starfish, fishes, shore birds, many others. Covers appearance, breeding, growth, feeding, much more. 305pp. 5¼ x 8¼. 23366-9

ATTRACTING BIRDS TO YOUR YARD, William J. Weber. Easy-to-follow guide offers advice on how to attract the greatest diversity of birds: birdhouses, feeders, water and waterers, much more. 96pp. 5³⁄₁₆ x 8¼. 28927-3

MEDICINAL AND OTHER USES OF NORTH AMERICAN PLANTS: A Historical Survey with Special Reference to the Eastern Indian Tribes, Charlotte Erichsen-Brown. Chronological historical citations document 500 years of usage of plants, trees, shrubs native to eastern Canada, northeastern U.S. Also complete identifying information. 343 illustrations. 544pp. 6½ x 9¼. 25951-X

STORYBOOK MAZES, Dave Phillips. 23 stories and mazes on two-page spreads: Wizard of Oz, Treasure Island, Robin Hood, etc. Solutions. 64pp. 8¼ x 11. 23628-5

AMERICAN NEGRO SONGS: 230 Folk Songs and Spirituals, Religious and Secular, John W. Work. This authoritative study traces the African influences of songs sung and played by black Americans at work, in church, and as entertainment. The author discusses the lyric significance of such songs as "Swing Low, Sweet Chariot," "John Henry," and others and offers the words and music for 230 songs. Bibliography. Index of Song Titles. 272pp. 6½ x 9¼. 40271-1

MOVIE-STAR PORTRAITS OF THE FORTIES, John Kobal (ed.). 163 glamor, studio photos of 106 stars of the 1940s: Rita Hayworth, Ava Gardner, Marlon Brando, Clark Gable, many more. 176pp. 8⅜ x 11¼. 23546-7

BENCHLEY LOST AND FOUND, Robert Benchley. Finest humor from early 30s, about pet peeves, child psychologists, post office and others. Mostly unavailable elsewhere. 73 illustrations by Peter Arno and others. 183pp. 5⅜ x 8½. 22410-4

YEKL and THE IMPORTED BRIDEGROOM AND OTHER STORIES OF YIDDISH NEW YORK, Abraham Cahan. Film Hester Street based on *Yekl* (1896). Novel, other stories among first about Jewish immigrants on N.Y.'s East Side. 240pp. 5⅜ x 8½. 22427-9

SELECTED POEMS, Walt Whitman. Generous sampling from *Leaves of Grass*. Twenty-four poems include "I Hear America Singing," "Song of the Open Road," "I Sing the Body Electric," "When Lilacs Last in the Dooryard Bloom'd," "O Captain! My Captain!"–all reprinted from an authoritative edition. Lists of titles and first lines. 128pp. 5³⁄₁₆ x 8¼. 26878-0

THE BEST TALES OF HOFFMANN, E. T. A. Hoffmann. 10 of Hoffmann's most important stories: "Nutcracker and the King of Mice," "The Golden Flowerpot," etc. 458pp. 5⅜ x 8½. 21793-0

FROM FETISH TO GOD IN ANCIENT EGYPT, E. A. Wallis Budge. Rich detailed survey of Egyptian conception of "God" and gods, magic, cult of animals, Osiris, more. Also, superb English translations of hymns and legends. 240 illustrations. 545pp. 5⅜ x 8½. 25803-3

FRENCH STORIES/CONTES FRANÇAIS: A Dual-Language Book, Wallace Fowlie. Ten stories by French masters, Voltaire to Camus: "Micromegas" by Voltaire; "The Atheist's Mass" by Balzac; "Minuet" by de Maupassant; "The Guest" by Camus, six more. Excellent English translations on facing pages. Also French-English vocabulary list, exercises, more. 352pp. 5⅜ x 8½. 26443-2

CHICAGO AT THE TURN OF THE CENTURY IN PHOTOGRAPHS: 122 Historic Views from the Collections of the Chicago Historical Society, Larry A. Viskochil. Rare large-format prints offer detailed views of City Hall, State Street, the Loop, Hull House, Union Station, many other landmarks, circa 1904-1913. Introduction. Captions. Maps. 144pp. 9⅜ x 12¼. 24656-6

OLD BROOKLYN IN EARLY PHOTOGRAPHS, 1865-1929, William Lee Younger. Luna Park, Gravesend race track, construction of Grand Army Plaza, moving of Hotel Brighton, etc. 157 previously unpublished photographs. 165pp. 8⅞ x 11¾. 23587-4

THE MYTHS OF THE NORTH AMERICAN INDIANS, Lewis Spence. Rich anthology of the myths and legends of the Algonquins, Iroquois, Pawnees and Sioux, prefaced by an extensive historical and ethnological commentary. 36 illustrations. 480pp. 5⅜ x 8½. 25967-6

AN ENCYCLOPEDIA OF BATTLES: Accounts of Over 1,560 Battles from 1479 B.C. to the Present, David Eggenberger. Essential details of every major battle in recorded history from the first battle of Megiddo in 1479 B.C. to Grenada in 1984. List of Battle Maps. New Appendix covering the years 1967-1984. Index. 99 illustrations. 544pp. 6½ x 9¼. 24913-1

SAILING ALONE AROUND THE WORLD, Captain Joshua Slocum. First man to sail around the world, alone, in small boat. One of great feats of seamanship told in delightful manner. 67 illustrations. 294pp. 5⅜ x 8½. 20326-3

ANARCHISM AND OTHER ESSAYS, Emma Goldman. Powerful, penetrating, prophetic essays on direct action, role of minorities, prison reform, puritan hypocrisy, violence, etc. 271pp. 5⅜ x 8½. 22484-8

MYTHS OF THE HINDUS AND BUDDHISTS, Ananda K. Coomaraswamy and Sister Nivedita. Great stories of the epics; deeds of Krishna, Shiva, taken from puranas, Vedas, folk tales; etc. 32 illustrations. 400pp. 5⅜ x 8½. 21759-0

THE TRAUMA OF BIRTH, Otto Rank. Rank's controversial thesis that anxiety neurosis is caused by profound psychological trauma which occurs at birth. 256pp. 5⅜ x 8½. 27974-X

A THEOLOGICO-POLITICAL TREATISE, Benedict Spinoza. Also contains unfinished Political Treatise. Great classic on religious liberty, theory of government on common consent. R. Elwes translation. Total of 421pp. 5⅜ x 8½. 20249-6

MY BONDAGE AND MY FREEDOM, Frederick Douglass. Born a slave, Douglass became outspoken force in antislavery movement. The best of Douglass' autobiographies. Graphic description of slave life. 464pp. 5⅜ x 8½. 22457-0

FOLLOWING THE EQUATOR: A Journey Around the World, Mark Twain. Fascinating humorous account of 1897 voyage to Hawaii, Australia, India, New Zealand, etc. Ironic, bemused reports on peoples, customs, climate, flora and fauna, politics, much more. 197 illustrations. 720pp. 5⅜ x 8½. 26113-1

THE PEOPLE CALLED SHAKERS, Edward D. Andrews. Definitive study of Shakers: origins, beliefs, practices, dances, social organization, furniture and crafts, etc. 33 illustrations. 351pp. 5⅜ x 8½. 21081-2

THE MYTHS OF GREECE AND ROME, H. A. Guerber. A classic of mythology, generously illustrated, long prized for its simple, graphic, accurate retelling of the principal myths of Greece and Rome, and for its commentary on their origins and significance. With 64 illustrations by Michelangelo, Raphael, Titian, Rubens, Canova, Bernini and others. 480pp. 5⅜ x 8½. 27584-1

PSYCHOLOGY OF MUSIC, Carl E. Seashore. Classic work discusses music as a medium from psychological viewpoint. Clear treatment of physical acoustics, auditory apparatus, sound perception, development of musical skills, nature of musical feeling, host of other topics. 88 figures. 408pp. 5⅜ x 8½. 21851-1

THE PHILOSOPHY OF HISTORY, Georg W. Hegel. Great classic of Western thought develops concept that history is not chance but rational process, the evolution of freedom. 457pp. 5⅜ x 8½. 20112-0

THE BOOK OF TEA, Kakuzo Okakura. Minor classic of the Orient: entertaining, charming explanation, interpretation of traditional Japanese culture in terms of tea ceremony. 94pp. 5⅜ x 8½. 20070-1

LIFE IN ANCIENT EGYPT, Adolf Erman. Fullest, most thorough, detailed older account with much not in more recent books, domestic life, religion, magic, medicine, commerce, much more. Many illustrations reproduce tomb paintings, carvings, hieroglyphs, etc. 597pp. 5⅜ x 8½. 22632-8

SUNDIALS, Their Theory and Construction, Albert Waugh. Far and away the best, most thorough coverage of ideas, mathematics concerned, types, construction, adjusting anywhere. Simple, nontechnical treatment allows even children to build several of these dials. Over 100 illustrations. 230pp. 5⅜ x 8½. 22947-5

THEORETICAL HYDRODYNAMICS, L. M. Milne-Thomson. Classic exposition of the mathematical theory of fluid motion, applicable to both hydrodynamics and aerodynamics. Over 600 exercises. 768pp. 6⅛ x 9¼. 68970-0

SONGS OF EXPERIENCE: Facsimile Reproduction with 26 Plates in Full Color, William Blake. 26 full-color plates from a rare 1826 edition. Includes "The Tyger," "London," "Holy Thursday," and other poems. Printed text of poems. 48pp. 5¼ x 7. 24636-1

OLD-TIME VIGNETTES IN FULL COLOR, Carol Belanger Grafton (ed.). Over 390 charming, often sentimental illustrations, selected from archives of Victorian graphics—pretty women posing, children playing, food, flowers, kittens and puppies, smiling cherubs, birds and butterflies, much more. All copyright-free. 48pp. 9¼ x 12¼. 27269-9

PERSPECTIVE FOR ARTISTS, Rex Vicat Cole. Depth, perspective of sky and sea, shadows, much more, not usually covered. 391 diagrams, 81 reproductions of drawings and paintings. 279pp. 5⅜ x 8½.   22487-2

DRAWING THE LIVING FIGURE, Joseph Sheppard. Innovative approach to artistic anatomy focuses on specifics of surface anatomy, rather than muscles and bones. Over 170 drawings of live models in front, back and side views, and in widely varying poses. Accompanying diagrams. 177 illustrations. Introduction. Index. 144pp. 8⅜ x11¼.   26723-7

GOTHIC AND OLD ENGLISH ALPHABETS: 100 Complete Fonts, Dan X. Solo. Add power, elegance to posters, signs, other graphics with 100 stunning copyright-free alphabets: Blackstone, Dolbey, Germania, 97 more—including many lower-case, numerals, punctuation marks. 104pp. 8⅛ x 11.   24695-7

HOW TO DO BEADWORK, Mary White. Fundamental book on craft from simple projects to five-bead chains and woven works. 106 illustrations. 142pp. 5⅜ x 8.
                                         20697-1

THE BOOK OF WOOD CARVING, Charles Marshall Sayers. Finest book for beginners discusses fundamentals and offers 34 designs. "Absolutely first rate . . . well thought out and well executed."–E. J. Tangerman. 118pp. 7¾ x 10⅝.   23654-4

ILLUSTRATED CATALOG OF CIVIL WAR MILITARY GOODS: Union Army Weapons, Insignia, Uniform Accessories, and Other Equipment, Schuyler, Hartley, and Graham. Rare, profusely illustrated 1846 catalog includes Union Army uniform and dress regulations, arms and ammunition, coats, insignia, flags, swords, rifles, etc. 226 illustrations. 160pp. 9 x 12.   24939-5

WOMEN'S FASHIONS OF THE EARLY 1900s: An Unabridged Republication of "New York Fashions, 1909," National Cloak & Suit Co. Rare catalog of mail-order fashions documents women's and children's clothing styles shortly after the turn of the century. Captions offer full descriptions, prices. Invaluable resource for fashion, costume historians. Approximately 725 illustrations. 128pp. 8⅜ x 11¼.   27276-1

THE 1912 AND 1915 GUSTAV STICKLEY FURNITURE CATALOGS, Gustav Stickley. With over 200 detailed illustrations and descriptions, these two catalogs are essential reading and reference materials and identification guides for Stickley furniture. Captions cite materials, dimensions and prices. 112pp. 6½ x 9¼.   26676-1

EARLY AMERICAN LOCOMOTIVES, John H. White, Jr. Finest locomotive engravings from early 19th century: historical (1804–74), main-line (after 1870), special, foreign, etc. 147 plates. 142pp. 11⅜ x 8¼.   22772-3

THE TALL SHIPS OF TODAY IN PHOTOGRAPHS, Frank O. Braynard. Lavishly illustrated tribute to nearly 100 majestic contemporary sailing vessels: Amerigo Vespucci, Clearwater, Constitution, Eagle, Mayflower, Sea Cloud, Victory, many more. Authoritative captions provide statistics, background on each ship. 190 black-and-white photographs and illustrations. Introduction. 128pp. 8⅞ x 11¾.
                                         27163-3

LITTLE BOOK OF EARLY AMERICAN CRAFTS AND TRADES, Peter Stockham (ed.). 1807 children's book explains crafts and trades: baker, hatter, cooper, potter, and many others. 23 copperplate illustrations. 140pp. 4⅝ x 6.   23336-7

VICTORIAN FASHIONS AND COSTUMES FROM HARPER'S BAZAR, 1867–1898, Stella Blum (ed.). Day costumes, evening wear, sports clothes, shoes, hats, other accessories in over 1,000 detailed engravings. 320pp. 9⅜ x 12¼.   22990-4

GUSTAV STICKLEY, THE CRAFTSMAN, Mary Ann Smith. Superb study surveys broad scope of Stickley's achievement, especially in architecture. Design philosophy, rise and fall of the Craftsman empire, descriptions and floor plans for many Craftsman houses, more. 86 black-and-white halftones. 31 line illustrations. Introduction 208pp. 6½ x 9¼.   27210-9

THE LONG ISLAND RAIL ROAD IN EARLY PHOTOGRAPHS, Ron Ziel. Over 220 rare photos, informative text document origin (1844) and development of rail service on Long Island. Vintage views of early trains, locomotives, stations, passengers, crews, much more. Captions. 8⅞ x 11¾.   26301-0

VOYAGE OF THE LIBERDADE, Joshua Slocum. Great 19th-century mariner's thrilling, first-hand account of the wreck of his ship off South America, the 35-foot boat he built from the wreckage, and its remarkable voyage home. 128pp. 5⅜ x 8½.   40022-0

TEN BOOKS ON ARCHITECTURE, Vitruvius. The most important book ever written on architecture. Early Roman aesthetics, technology, classical orders, site selection, all other aspects. Morgan translation. 331pp. 5⅜ x 8½.   20645-9

THE HUMAN FIGURE IN MOTION, Eadweard Muybridge. More than 4,500 stopped-action photos, in action series, showing undraped men, women, children jumping, lying down, throwing, sitting, wrestling, carrying, etc. 390pp. 7⅞ x 10⅝.   20204-6 Clothbd.

TREES OF THE EASTERN AND CENTRAL UNITED STATES AND CANADA, William M. Harlow. Best one-volume guide to 140 trees. Full descriptions, woodlore, range, etc. Over 600 illustrations. Handy size. 288pp. 4½ x 6⅜.   20395-6

SONGS OF WESTERN BIRDS, Dr. Donald J. Borror. Complete song and call repertoire of 60 western species, including flycatchers, juncoes, cactus wrens, many more–includes fully illustrated booklet.   Cassette and manual 99913-0

GROWING AND USING HERBS AND SPICES, Milo Miloradovich. Versatile handbook provides all the information needed for cultivation and use of all the herbs and spices available in North America. 4 illustrations. Index. Glossary. 236pp. 5⅜ x 8½.   25058-X

BIG BOOK OF MAZES AND LABYRINTHS, Walter Shepherd. 50 mazes and labyrinths in all–classical, solid, ripple, and more–in one great volume. Perfect inexpensive puzzler for clever youngsters. Full solutions. 112pp. 8⅛ x 11.   22951-3

PIANO TUNING, J. Cree Fischer. Clearest, best book for beginner, amateur. Simple repairs, raising dropped notes, tuning by easy method of flattened fifths. No previous skills needed. 4 illustrations. 201pp. 5⅜ x 8½. 23267-0

HINTS TO SINGERS, Lillian Nordica. Selecting the right teacher, developing confidence, overcoming stage fright, and many other important skills receive thoughtful discussion in this indispensible guide, written by a world-famous diva of four decades' experience. 96pp. 5⅜ x 8½. 40094-8

THE COMPLETE NONSENSE OF EDWARD LEAR, Edward Lear. All nonsense limericks, zany alphabets, Owl and Pussycat, songs, nonsense botany, etc., illustrated by Lear. Total of 320pp. 5⅜ x 8½. (Available in U.S. only.) 20167-8

VICTORIAN PARLOUR POETRY: An Annotated Anthology, Michael R. Turner. 117 gems by Longfellow, Tennyson, Browning, many lesser-known poets. "The Village Blacksmith," "Curfew Must Not Ring Tonight," "Only a Baby Small," dozens more, often difficult to find elsewhere. Index of poets, titles, first lines. xxiii + 325pp. 5⅝ x 8¼. 27044-0

DUBLINERS, James Joyce. Fifteen stories offer vivid, tightly focused observations of the lives of Dublin's poorer classes. At least one, "The Dead," is considered a masterpiece. Reprinted complete and unabridged from standard edition. 160pp. 5$\frac{3}{16}$ x 8¼. 26870-5

GREAT WEIRD TALES: 14 Stories by Lovecraft, Blackwood, Machen and Others, S. T. Joshi (ed.). 14 spellbinding tales, including "The Sin Eater," by Fiona McLeod, "The Eye Above the Mantel," by Frank Belknap Long, as well as renowned works by R. H. Barlow, Lord Dunsany, Arthur Machen, W. C. Morrow and eight other masters of the genre. 256pp. 5⅜ x 8½. (Available in U.S. only.) 40436-6

THE BOOK OF THE SACRED MAGIC OF ABRAMELIN THE MAGE, translated by S. MacGregor Mathers. Medieval manuscript of ceremonial magic. Basic document in Aleister Crowley, Golden Dawn groups. 268pp. 5⅜ x 8½. 23211-5

NEW RUSSIAN-ENGLISH AND ENGLISH-RUSSIAN DICTIONARY, M. A. O'Brien. This is a remarkably handy Russian dictionary, containing a surprising amount of information, including over 70,000 entries. 366pp. 4½ x 6⅛. 20208-9

HISTORIC HOMES OF THE AMERICAN PRESIDENTS, Second, Revised Edition, Irvin Haas. A traveler's guide to American Presidential homes, most open to the public, depicting and describing homes occupied by every American President from George Washington to George Bush. With visiting hours, admission charges, travel routes. 175 photographs. Index. 160pp. 8¼ x 11. 26751-2

NEW YORK IN THE FORTIES, Andreas Feininger. 162 brilliant photographs by the well-known photographer, formerly with *Life* magazine. Commuters, shoppers, Times Square at night, much else from city at its peak. Captions by John von Hartz. 181pp. 9¼ x 10¾. 23585-8

INDIAN SIGN LANGUAGE, William Tomkins. Over 525 signs developed by Sioux and other tribes. Written instructions and diagrams. Also 290 pictographs. 111pp. 6⅛ x 9¼. 22029-X

ANATOMY: A Complete Guide for Artists, Joseph Sheppard. A master of figure drawing shows artists how to render human anatomy convincingly. Over 460 illustrations. 224pp. 8⅜ x 11¼. 27279-6

MEDIEVAL CALLIGRAPHY: Its History and Technique, Marc Drogin. Spirited history, comprehensive instruction manual covers 13 styles (ca. 4th century through 15th). Excellent photographs; directions for duplicating medieval techniques with modern tools. 224pp. 8⅜ x 11¼. 26142-5

DRIED FLOWERS: How to Prepare Them, Sarah Whitlock and Martha Rankin. Complete instructions on how to use silica gel, meal and borax, perlite aggregate, sand and borax, glycerine and water to create attractive permanent flower arrangements. 12 illustrations. 32pp. 5⅜ x 8½. 21802-3

EASY-TO-MAKE BIRD FEEDERS FOR WOODWORKERS, Scott D. Campbell. Detailed, simple-to-use guide for designing, constructing, caring for and using feeders. Text, illustrations for 12 classic and contemporary designs. 96pp. 5⅜ x 8½. 25847-5

SCOTTISH WONDER TALES FROM MYTH AND LEGEND, Donald A. Mackenzie. 16 lively tales tell of giants rumbling down mountainsides, of a magic wand that turns stone pillars into warriors, of gods and goddesses, evil hags, powerful forces and more. 240pp. 5⅜ x 8½. 29677-6

THE HISTORY OF UNDERCLOTHES, C. Willett Cunnington and Phyllis Cunnington. Fascinating, well-documented survey covering six centuries of English undergarments, enhanced with over 100 illustrations: 12th-century laced-up bodice, footed long drawers (1795), 19th-century bustles, 19th-century corsets for men, Victorian "bust improvers," much more. 272pp. 5⅜ x 8¼. 27124-2

ARTS AND CRAFTS FURNITURE: The Complete Brooks Catalog of 1912, Brooks Manufacturing Co. Photos and detailed descriptions of more than 150 now very collectible furniture designs from the Arts and Crafts movement depict davenports, settees, buffets, desks, tables, chairs, bedsteads, dressers and more, all built of solid, quarter-sawed oak. Invaluable for students and enthusiasts of antiques, Americana and the decorative arts. 80pp. 6½ x 9¼. 27471-3

WILBUR AND ORVILLE: A Biography of the Wright Brothers, Fred Howard. Definitive, crisply written study tells the full story of the brothers' lives and work. A vividly written biography, unparalleled in scope and color, that also captures the spirit of an extraordinary era. 560pp. 6⅛ x 9¼. 40297-5

THE ARTS OF THE SAILOR: Knotting, Splicing and Ropework, Hervey Garrett Smith. Indispensable shipboard reference covers tools, basic knots and useful hitches; handsewing and canvas work, more. Over 100 illustrations. Delightful reading for sea lovers. 256pp. 5⅜ x 8½. 26440-8

FRANK LLOYD WRIGHT'S FALLINGWATER: The House and Its History, Second, Revised Edition, Donald Hoffmann. A total revision—both in text and illustrations—of the standard document on Fallingwater, the boldest, most personal architectural statement of Wright's mature years, updated with valuable new material from the recently opened Frank Lloyd Wright Archives. "Fascinating"—*The New York Times*. 116 illustrations. 128pp. 9¼ x 10¾. 27430-6

PHOTOGRAPHIC SKETCHBOOK OF THE CIVIL WAR, Alexander Gardner. 100 photos taken on field during the Civil War. Famous shots of Manassas Harper's Ferry, Lincoln, Richmond, slave pens, etc. 244pp. 10⅝ x 8¼.   22731-6

FIVE ACRES AND INDEPENDENCE, Maurice G. Kains. Great back-to-the-land classic explains basics of self-sufficient farming. The one book to get. 95 illustrations. 397pp. 5⅜ x 8½.   20974-1

SONGS OF EASTERN BIRDS, Dr. Donald J. Borror. Songs and calls of 60 species most common to eastern U.S.: warblers, woodpeckers, flycatchers, thrushes, larks, many more in high-quality recording.   Cassette and manual 99912-2

A MODERN HERBAL, Margaret Grieve. Much the fullest, most exact, most useful compilation of herbal material. Gigantic alphabetical encyclopedia, from aconite to zedoary, gives botanical information, medical properties, folklore, economic uses, much else. Indispensable to serious reader. 161 illustrations. 888pp. 6½ x 9¼. 2-vol. set. (Available in U.S. only.)
Vol. I: 22798-7
Vol. II: 22799-5

HIDDEN TREASURE MAZE BOOK, Dave Phillips. Solve 34 challenging mazes accompanied by heroic tales of adventure. Evil dragons, people-eating plants, bloodthirsty giants, many more dangerous adversaries lurk at every twist and turn. 34 mazes, stories, solutions. 48pp. 8¼ x 11.   24566-7

LETTERS OF W. A. MOZART, Wolfgang A. Mozart. Remarkable letters show bawdy wit, humor, imagination, musical insights, contemporary musical world; includes some letters from Leopold Mozart. 276pp. 5⅜ x 8½.   22859-2

BASIC PRINCIPLES OF CLASSICAL BALLET, Agrippina Vaganova. Great Russian theoretician, teacher explains methods for teaching classical ballet. 118 illustrations. 175pp. 5⅜ x 8½.   22036-2

THE JUMPING FROG, Mark Twain. Revenge edition. The original story of The Celebrated Jumping Frog of Calaveras County, a hapless French translation, and Twain's hilarious "retranslation" from the French. 12 illustrations. 66pp. 5⅜ x 8½.   22686-7

BEST REMEMBERED POEMS, Martin Gardner (ed.). The 126 poems in this superb collection of 19th- and 20th-century British and American verse range from Shelley's "To a Skylark" to the impassioned "Renascence" of Edna St. Vincent Millay and to Edward Lear's whimsical "The Owl and the Pussycat." 224pp. 5⅜ x 8½.   27165-X

COMPLETE SONNETS, William Shakespeare. Over 150 exquisite poems deal with love, friendship, the tyranny of time, beauty's evanescence, death and other themes in language of remarkable power, precision and beauty. Glossary of archaic terms. 80pp. 5³⁄₁₆ x 8¼.   26686-9

THE BATTLES THAT CHANGED HISTORY, Fletcher Pratt. Eminent historian profiles 16 crucial conflicts, ancient to modern, that changed the course of civilization. 352pp. 5⅜ x 8½.   41129-X

THE WIT AND HUMOR OF OSCAR WILDE, Alvin Redman (ed.). More than 1,000 ripostes, paradoxes, wisecracks: Work is the curse of the drinking classes; I can resist everything except temptation; etc. 258pp. $5\frac{3}{8}$ x $8\frac{1}{2}$. 20602-5

SHAKESPEARE LEXICON AND QUOTATION DICTIONARY, Alexander Schmidt. Full definitions, locations, shades of meaning in every word in plays and poems. More than 50,000 exact quotations. 1,485pp. $6\frac{1}{2}$ x $9\frac{1}{4}$. 2-vol. set.
Vol. 1: 22726-X
Vol. 2: 22727-8

SELECTED POEMS, Emily Dickinson. Over 100 best-known, best-loved poems by one of America's foremost poets, reprinted from authoritative early editions. No comparable edition at this price. Index of first lines. 64pp. $5\frac{3}{16}$ x $8\frac{1}{4}$. 26466-1

THE INSIDIOUS DR. FU-MANCHU, Sax Rohmer. The first of the popular mystery series introduces a pair of English detectives to their archnemesis, the diabolical Dr. Fu-Manchu. Flavorful atmosphere, fast-paced action, and colorful characters enliven this classic of the genre. 208pp. $5\frac{3}{16}$ x $8\frac{1}{4}$. 29898-1

THE MALLEUS MALEFICARUM OF KRAMER AND SPRENGER, translated by Montague Summers. Full text of most important witchhunter's "bible," used by both Catholics and Protestants. 278pp. $6\frac{5}{8}$ x 10. 22802-9

SPANISH STORIES/CUENTOS ESPAÑOLES: A Dual-Language Book, Angel Flores (ed.). Unique format offers 13 great stories in Spanish by Cervantes, Borges, others. Faithful English translations on facing pages. 352pp. $5\frac{3}{8}$ x $8\frac{1}{2}$. 25399-6

GARDEN CITY, LONG ISLAND, IN EARLY PHOTOGRAPHS, 1869–1919, Mildred H. Smith. Handsome treasury of 118 vintage pictures, accompanied by carefully researched captions, document the Garden City Hotel fire (1899), the Vanderbilt Cup Race (1908), the first airmail flight departing from the Nassau Boulevard Aerodrome (1911), and much more. 96pp. $8\frac{7}{8}$ x $11\frac{3}{4}$. 40669-5

OLD QUEENS, N.Y., IN EARLY PHOTOGRAPHS, Vincent F. Seyfried and William Asadorian. Over 160 rare photographs of Maspeth, Jamaica, Jackson Heights, and other areas. Vintage views of DeWitt Clinton mansion, 1939 World's Fair and more. Captions. 192pp. $8\frac{7}{8}$ x 11. 26358-4

CAPTURED BY THE INDIANS: 15 Firsthand Accounts, 1750-1870, Frederick Drimmer. Astounding true historical accounts of grisly torture, bloody conflicts, relentless pursuits, miraculous escapes and more, by people who lived to tell the tale. 384pp. $5\frac{3}{8}$ x $8\frac{1}{2}$. 24901-8

THE WORLD'S GREAT SPEECHES (Fourth Enlarged Edition), Lewis Copeland, Lawrence W. Lamm, and Stephen J. McKenna. Nearly 300 speeches provide public speakers with a wealth of updated quotes and inspiration–from Pericles' funeral oration and William Jennings Bryan's "Cross of Gold Speech" to Malcolm X's powerful words on the Black Revolution and Earl of Spenser's tribute to his sister, Diana, Princess of Wales. 944pp. $5\frac{3}{8}$ x $8\frac{3}{8}$. 40903-1

THE BOOK OF THE SWORD, Sir Richard F. Burton. Great Victorian scholar/adventurer's eloquent, erudite history of the "queen of weapons"–from prehistory to early Roman Empire. Evolution and development of early swords, variations (sabre, broadsword, cutlass, scimitar, etc.), much more. 336pp. $6\frac{1}{8}$ x $9\frac{1}{4}$. 25434-8

AUTOBIOGRAPHY: The Story of My Experiments with Truth, Mohandas K. Gandhi. Boyhood, legal studies, purification, the growth of the Satyagraha (nonviolent protest) movement. Critical, inspiring work of the man responsible for the freedom of India. 480pp. 5⅜ x 8½. (Available in U.S. only.) 24593-4

CELTIC MYTHS AND LEGENDS, T. W. Rolleston. Masterful retelling of Irish and Welsh stories and tales. Cuchulain, King Arthur, Deirdre, the Grail, many more. First paperback edition. 58 full-page illustrations. 512pp. 5⅜ x 8½. 26507-2

THE PRINCIPLES OF PSYCHOLOGY, William James. Famous long course complete, unabridged. Stream of thought, time perception, memory, experimental methods; great work decades ahead of its time. 94 figures. 1,391pp. 5⅜ x 8½. 2-vol. set.
Vol. I: 20381-6 Vol. II: 20382-4

THE WORLD AS WILL AND REPRESENTATION, Arthur Schopenhauer. Definitive English translation of Schopenhauer's life work, correcting more than 1,000 errors, omissions in earlier translations. Translated by E. F. J. Payne. Total of 1,269pp. 5⅜ x 8½. 2-vol. set. Vol. 1: 21761-2 Vol. 2: 21762-0

MAGIC AND MYSTERY IN TIBET, Madame Alexandra David-Neel. Experiences among lamas, magicians, sages, sorcerers, Bonpa wizards. A true psychic discovery. 32 illustrations. 321pp. 5⅜ x 8½. (Available in U.S. only.) 22682-4

THE EGYPTIAN BOOK OF THE DEAD, E. A. Wallis Budge. Complete reproduction of Ani's papyrus, finest ever found. Full hieroglyphic text, interlinear transliteration, word-for-word translation, smooth translation. 533pp. 6½ x 9¼. 21866-X

MATHEMATICS FOR THE NONMATHEMATICIAN, Morris Kline. Detailed, college-level treatment of mathematics in cultural and historical context, with numerous exercises. Recommended Reading Lists. Tables. Numerous figures. 641pp. 5⅜ x 8½.
24823-2

PROBABILISTIC METHODS IN THE THEORY OF STRUCTURES, Isaac Elishakoff. Well-written introduction covers the elements of the theory of probability from two or more random variables, the reliability of such multivariable structures, the theory of random function, Monte Carlo methods of treating problems incapable of exact solution, and more. Examples. 502pp. 5⅜ x 8½. 40691-1

THE RIME OF THE ANCIENT MARINER, Gustave Doré, S. T. Coleridge. Doré's finest work; 34 plates capture moods, subtleties of poem. Flawless full-size reproductions printed on facing pages with authoritative text of poem. "Beautiful. Simply beautiful."–*Publisher's Weekly.* 77pp. 9¼ x 12. 22305-1

NORTH AMERICAN INDIAN DESIGNS FOR ARTISTS AND CRAFTSPEOPLE, Eva Wilson. Over 360 authentic copyright-free designs adapted from Navajo blankets, Hopi pottery, Sioux buffalo hides, more. Geometrics, symbolic figures, plant and animal motifs, etc. 128pp. 8⅜ x 11. (Not for sale in the United Kingdom.) 25341-4

SCULPTURE: Principles and Practice, Louis Slobodkin. Step-by-step approach to clay, plaster, metals, stone; classical and modern. 253 drawings, photos. 255pp. 8⅛ x 11.
22960-2

THE INFLUENCE OF SEA POWER UPON HISTORY, 1660–1783, A. T. Mahan. Influential classic of naval history and tactics still used as text in war colleges. First paperback edition. 4 maps. 24 battle plans. 640pp. 5⅜ x 8½. 25509-3

CATALOG OF DOVER BOOKS

THE STORY OF THE TITANIC AS TOLD BY ITS SURVIVORS, Jack Winocour (ed.). What it was really like. Panic, despair, shocking inefficiency, and a little heroism. More thrilling than any fictional account. 26 illustrations. 320pp. 5⅜ x 8½.
20610-6

FAIRY AND FOLK TALES OF THE IRISH PEASANTRY, William Butler Yeats (ed.). Treasury of 64 tales from the twilight world of Celtic myth and legend: "The Soul Cages," "The Kildare Pooka," "King O'Toole and his Goose," many more. Introduction and Notes by W. B. Yeats. 352pp. 5⅜ x 8½.
26941-8

BUDDHIST MAHAYANA TEXTS, E. B. Cowell and others (eds.). Superb, accurate translations of basic documents in Mahayana Buddhism, highly important in history of religions. The Buddha-karita of Asvaghosha, Larger Sukhavativyuha, more. 448pp. 5⅜ x 8½.
25552-2

ONE TWO THREE . . . INFINITY: Facts and Speculations of Science, George Gamow. Great physicist's fascinating, readable overview of contemporary science: number theory, relativity, fourth dimension, entropy, genes, atomic structure, much more. 128 illustrations. Index. 352pp. 5⅜ x 8½.
25664-2

EXPERIMENTATION AND MEASUREMENT, W. J. Youden. Introductory manual explains laws of measurement in simple terms and offers tips for achieving accuracy and minimizing errors. Mathematics of measurement, use of instruments, experimenting with machines. 1994 edition. Foreword. Preface. Introduction. Epilogue. Selected Readings. Glossary. Index. Tables and figures. 128pp. 5⅜ x 8½.
40451-X

DALÍ ON MODERN ART: The Cuckolds of Antiquated Modern Art, Salvador Dalí. Influential painter skewers modern art and its practitioners. Outrageous evaluations of Picasso, Cézanne, Turner, more. 15 renderings of paintings discussed. 44 calligraphic decorations by Dalí. 96pp. 5⅜ x 8½. (Available in U.S. only.)
29220-7

ANTIQUE PLAYING CARDS: A Pictorial History, Henry René D'Allemagne. Over 900 elaborate, decorative images from rare playing cards (14th–20th centuries): Bacchus, death, dancing dogs, hunting scenes, royal coats of arms, players cheating, much more. 96pp. 9¼ x 12¼.
29265-7

MAKING FURNITURE MASTERPIECES: 30 Projects with Measured Drawings, Franklin H. Gottshall. Step-by-step instructions, illustrations for constructing handsome, useful pieces, among them a Sheraton desk, Chippendale chair, Spanish desk, Queen Anne table and a William and Mary dressing mirror. 224pp. 8⅛ x 11¼.
29338-6

THE FOSSIL BOOK: A Record of Prehistoric Life, Patricia V. Rich et al. Profusely illustrated definitive guide covers everything from single-celled organisms and dinosaurs to birds and mammals and the interplay between climate and man. Over 1,500 illustrations. 760pp. 7½ x 10⅛.
29371-8